WITH WANDERING STEPS & SLOW

Growing toward God

JOY HOFFMAN

InterVarsity Press
Downers Grove
Illinois 60515

InterVarsity Press is the book-publishing division of Inter-Varsity Christian Fellowship, a student movement active on campus at hundreds of universities, colleges and schools of nursing. For information about local and regional activities, write IVCF, 233 Langdon St., Madison, WI 53703.

Distributed in Canada through InterVarsity Press, 1875 Leslie St., Unit 10, Don Mills, Ontario M3B 2M5, Canada.

ISBN 0-87784-804-1

Printed in the United States of America

Library of Congress Cataloging in Publication Data
Hoffman, Joy, 1954-
    With wandering steps and slow.

    1. Hoffman, Joy, 1954-   . 2. Christian
biography—United States. 3. Christian life—
1960-   . I. Title.
BR1725.H625A38   280'.4'0924 [B]   81-18566
ISBN 0-87784-804-1   AACR2

17	16	15	14	13	12	11	10	9	8	7	6	5	4	3	2	1
96	95	94	93	92	91	90	89	88	87	86	85	84	83	82		

The world was all before them, where to choose
Their place of rest, and Providence their guide;
They hand in hand, with wandering steps and slow,
Through Eden took their solitary way.

Milton/Paradise Lost 12. 646-649

PREFACE

I thank with all my heart those mentors who have nurtured and loved me throughout the course of my Christian pilgrimage: Tom and Edna Manetsch, Sr. Francine Danis, Sr. Mary Mark Mylod, and the Rev. Don Allen. I am also very grateful to Chuck Neufeld of Mennonite Voluntary Service for having the grace to accept the writing of this book as a project worthy of his support.

Though some details have been altered, the story told here is true. I thank "Hope" and "Mark" for having the courage to share it.

Joy Hoffman

I
THE DEBT IMMENSE

The debt immense of endless gratitude...

Milton/Paradise Lost 4. 52

November 3, 1976

Dr. Mark Boswell
Sanctuary
222 North O'Hara
Cedar Valley, Pennsylvania

Dear Dr. Boswell:

Fall is taking its last breath here in Michigan. As I look out my window, I see the sun succumbing reluctantly to the cold and darkness. There's Mozart playing on my radio—*Eine Kleine Nachtmusik*, appropriately. It seems that night is coming all around me, except in my heart. And that's why I have been thinking of you the last few days and have finally summoned the courage to write. I hope that I am not violating some doctor/patient etiquette. Of course, you are not my doctor anymore, but that curious distance that must be maintained for clinical purposes still prevents me from feeling completely at ease with you, even in a letter.

Yet I so much want to tell you that I am fine. Really fine. Was it only eight months ago that we sat together in that room in Kramer Hall with the beige plaster cracking around the curtainless windows? So short a time since I was wringing my hands around a wet Kleenex, crying out to you that my life had fallen apart? Even now I remember so vividly being doped on those big white 50-milligram thunderbolts, lying in bed biting the sheet and begging my roommate to manufacture some stories about why I wasn't going to class. I always wondered if you had contempt for me then, you so big and strong with your omniscient blue-eyed gazes. I wondered if you were as godlike as I perceived you, or if you had ever stumbled too. No matter. I'm in no need of gods now. These last two months have shown me how many opportunities are ahead and how I can take care of myself just fine. Graduate school is a delightful place, and I am having a good time here!

At first it was a jolt to go from the tiny, womblike cocoon of Harrisville College to a huge, cosmopolitan university like this. On my first day here I actually got lost. The place is simply enormous. The graduate student dormitory where I live has more people in it than Harrisville's entire student body. Believe me, I spent a long time depressed by the sheer impersonality of it, about strolling across campus and never meeting a single person to say hi to. Most of all, I was depressed that no one here knew or cared about my distinguished undergraduate career. I found myself a nobody. I wanted to back away, and all the lessons you tried to teach me about confidence and self-esteem disintegrated. Crying in my room with a bottle of cheap wine to keep me company, I did a pretty good job of convincing myself that I'd be a complete failure.

On top of all that, my assistantship turned out to be a teaching rather than a research assignment. *Teaching*. I was all set to delve into the library stacks, but instead was dispatched to a place called the English Language Center, which gives foreign students instruction in basic language skills. Instead of confronting Shakespeare and Plato, I came face to face with a crowd of Arabs, Iranians, Japanese, Brazilians and Indonesians who could do no

13

more than say yes, no and Coca-Cola. On my first day in class I wanted to die. I'd never studied anything even remotely connected to education or psychology.

But slowly, in the midst of all this, I sensed that I had come to the right place. I began to make a little progress with the students and to actually care about their great problems and needs. Not that I will ever be a great teacher—you and I both know I don't have what it takes —but I can get through my allotted hour without collapsing and can sometimes reach out to them in their homesickness and vulnerability. Nor do I want to abandon them until I have tried my best. Do you Christians have a fancy word for this sense of *rightness?* No doubt you call it Providence; I call it getting lucky.

In addition, I'm enjoying the academic work. I've also begun counseling with a woman psychologist named Sarah. I see her an hour a week, and she and I are building on the foundation I laid with you. She helps me to see better why I act the way I do and how to get more control over it. That's important for teaching. How clearly I remember you saying that I'd be a rotten teacher and scholar because I refused to give of myself! You were right. Learning to give is painful and scary. But I am making a bit of progress. The students have so many needs that I am forced to give to them.

I've learned to appreciate the sheer space and great beauty of this campus, and to dabble in the many cultural advantages that were simply nonexistent in Harrisville. So it is not at all bad here. I want to do well in my studies, but I doubt that I would ever try to take my own life again if I don't succeed. The accepting, less hectic, sprawling Midwestern environment is like a tonic. Or maybe I'm just growing up. Or maybe I'm being lulled by this indescribable certainty I have that I have come to the right place. Whatever the answer, I have you to thank, for you reached out to me when there was no one else to care and helped put the pieces back together. I will keep you posted. For now, suffice it to say that all is calm in Michigan—and that autumn has brought my springtime.

Sincerely,
Hope Martin

December 14, 1976

Ms. Hope Martin
E 565 Graduate Hall
College Park, Michigan

Dear Hope:

Thank you for taking the time to write. It sounds like you are doing some tremendous developing, and I'm delighted by your experiences. You are discovering you have more assets than you ever dreamed possible. I have no idea where you will ultimately find your niche in life, but I'm pleased that you are learning to deal with new experiences so positively. It's exciting, too, that you can explore new possibilities without putting yourself down so much.

What excites me most, Hope, is that I have been able to be a part of your life and that somehow I have helped to make it better for you. We just needed to take the cap off the wellspring of your personality so that your beauty could begin to flow. Your students probably see in you a great deal more warmth and sensitivity than you will admit to.

I'm pleased that you felt comfortable enough with counseling to continue with it. Seeing someone who is both aggressive and caring will be very good. I hope that you continue that relationship until the two of you agree that a break is appropriate. I continue to counsel students at Harrisville, and my practice here at the hospital gets more hectic each day. Sometimes I feel like I am going

16

through a revolving door, that I haven't enough time to do high-quality work, but I still enjoy my work totally. When I get letters from people like you, I am thrilled by what can happen in people's lives. This encourages me to press on. The words of someone struggling to grow and to handle life a bit more responsibly both strengthen me and shake me out of my fatigue.

I am delighted to hear of your development. Thank you for encouraging me and sharing your growth with me. I hope that you will continue to keep me informed about the new directions in which your life is going.

Warmest regards,
Mark Boswell
Chief of Psychology

January 27, 1977

Dear Dr. Boswell:

Your letter was very kind. Thank you for writing it. I am mystified by your claim to see a great beauty in me. I don't feel very beautiful, and I think my other letter to you was euphoric and stupid. How shallow my illusions of self-control were! I feel like a baby these days, troubled and confused by an ambiguous world that is too large for me. There is no one to confide in except my counselor, and I'm not even sure how far I trust her, for she encourages me to do things that don't seem right. As you know, I have never had any really intimate friends, and now I need a listening ear so badly. Do you mind if I turn to you now, just for a little while? Can you guide me again as you once did?

Throughout our sessions together, did you ever sense that all of the experiences common to a fourteen-year-old were still ahead of me? That I had postponed my adolescence? Sometimes I think that about myself. I've been so serious and responsible all my life that I have little knowledge of how to loosen up, how to play. I always practiced my music diligently, brought home splendid report cards and read three books a week. But I was an utter failure in gym class and the last to be chosen for games on the playground. Now, all at once I find myself in a university where people are having good times that I never learned how to have. Nobody here spends Friday and Saturday night in the library or commends me if I do.

To conquer the insecurity I am feeling, my counselor has encouraged me to go to parties and dances. Never in my whole life have I been to a dance, a prom or anything like that. I've never even danced with a man. At 22, I should have done that, don't you think? Perhaps I wouldn't feel so out of it now if I had. I have forced myself to go to some social activities here, but I feel so awkward and misplaced that I just end up getting drunk because there is nothing else to do. Everybody around me seems relaxed, rowdy and fun-loving, but I don't know how to enter into the spirit of that fun. And I'm so unattractive that people hardly flock to me.

So I ask myself—why don't I just concentrate on my books and my scholarly inquiry, do what I do best, instead of subjecting myself to the agonies of social encounters? Well, I would, I honestly would flee right over to the research stacks and bury myself, except for this overwhelming sense I have that something is missing from my life. There's a whole dimension of experience that I missed somewhere on the way to academic greatness. What am I looking for? Social life is the answer I keep coming up with. I now have everything I thought I was striving for—important work to do, a wonderful university environment, enough money to live comfortably—but it isn't enough. I am hungry for people, for a social identity.

But social life isn't all that it's cracked up to be. Maybe I say this because I simply haven't the skills to manage it. Let me give you an example. Last weekend I went to a dorm dance. I sat in a corner for a while, and then a good-looking foreign student came over and asked me to dance. I was surprised, considering my weight problem, that he had even looked twice at me. But I stumbled out onto the floor with him, waved my arms around and tried to dance. Then we sat down and he kept giving me beer, and I kept drinking it because I didn't know what to say to him. (Funny, if he had been one of my students, I could have talked to him all night. I was just so unsure of myself in this new social role that I was tongue-tied.) Finally he suggested that we walk back to my room. Because I was a little unsteady by that time, he took my arm and guided me along. The next thing I knew, the door of my room was locked behind us, I had been pushed up against the wall, and this strange man whose name I couldn't even remember was breathing all over me and telling me how much he wanted me. It was horrible, because I was so unprepared for it. I had no precedent. My shock suddenly turned into a torrent of tears, which apparently scared him enough that he left.

I made a complete fool of myself. It occurs to me that his intentions at that dance would have been obvious to any teen-ager, but didn't register with me because I'm such a klutz and social moron. My question is—what can I do about it? Have I hopelessly warped myself through all the years of acting older than my age? Has part of my life passed me by forever, a part that I will always long for but can no longer get hold of? I have missed something. I feel cheated and bereft, and can't even put a name to the thing I yearn for. Community... an end to my isolation... comfort... rest. It's all of those.

As I consider that last paragraph, I am almost afraid of what you are going to reply. I implore you, even though you are a Christian and even though Sanctuary is a Christian hospital, please don't give me Billy-Graham-ish answers. I've read Augustine and Luther, but I have also read Nietzsche and Sartre, and I know going to church won't do anything for me. I went to church for years and heard empty sermons that only increased my own emptiness. I'm finished with all that. I want to hear something new, something that is psychologically respectable.

My sentences are badly written and poorly organized, perhaps mirroring the tumult within. Can you restore some balance? I almost wish that we were together again in our cracked-plaster room, so that you could take my broken parts and glue them together again.

Imploringly,
Hope

February 20, 1977

Dear Hope,

Therapy-by-mail is a little unusual for me, but I will do my best to cope with some of the questions you have raised. I am glad that you trust me enough to confide in me. I don't know if my responses will be of much use to you, but I hope that they will provide a little warmth in this very cold winter.

You have within you great social gifts that you have not yet begun to develop. I don't know if it's useful to speak of them in terms of postponed adolescence. Do you really think you would be a better person now if you had attended a prom or learned to dance five years ago? Hope, you are buying in pretty uncritically to the norms of the culture around you, the norms that dictate what must happen when. In many cultures women don't even begin to date until they are in their twenties. There is nothing wrong with you, nor are you hopelessly backward. Rather, think about the terrain you have to explore in the years ahead, and about the maturity you have to make that exploration more complete and satisfying. Your confusion when the man entered your room stemmed only from inexperience, not from clumsiness, and inexperience need carry no value judgment. Why do you insist on condemning yourself? You know deep down that you didn't want the casual, ephemeral contact he was offering. Yet you almost seem to be trying to convince yourself you did want it.

No, the words you use to describe your need

are the big words: rest, consolation, community. Your remarks about feeling cheated and bereft of something are much closer to the mark than your fears about going to parties. You are far enough along in your journey of self-discovery to know that you cannot lay all these feelings squarely at your parents' door. I wish with all my heart that they had known how to love you better, but the past is past. You are *you* now, not just their offspring. As *you*, you need to make your own decisions and take responsibility for them.

So where can we look for the key to your feeling of having missed out on something? Doesn't the defensive tone of the last paragraph of your letter betray you? You beg me to tell you something new, but you well know that there is nothing new under the sun. The very fact that you chose to write your letter to me instead of someone else gives you away. How desperately your heart and mind and soul are crying for rest. Why do you fight it so hard? I know that you have read all the theologians and philosophers and could quote them to me for hours, could point out their excesses and inconsistencies, as though your act of criticism would ease the pain of your all-too-real emotional hurts. You have wrestled with Calvin and Aquinas and Kierkegaard. But I do not hear you talking about confronting Jesus Christ the way you have confronted some of his disciples and detractors.

For years you have let your extraordinary intellectual gifts imprison you instead of free you, by putting up walls of objections and criticism against the very thing that will heal you. Please believe that I do not say that to hurt you. I think you want me to say it. Don't you,

23

in your heart of hearts, long for him? Are you satisfied with your collection of doubts? Have you really given him a chance? I don't mean have you given the ontological proof or the Heidelberg Catechism a chance. Have you given the living, loving Christ a chance to hold you in his arms and tell you that all will be well?

As a first-rate scholar, you know that you must search for truth no matter where that search takes you. I challenge you now to look for the truth about what is troubling you, and not to rule out anything until you give it serious and objective consideration. You have investigated dancing and drinking and studying, and none has filled you. The teaching and the reputation you built do not supply your needs either. You owe it to yourself to seek the answer, wherever it lies. You know this. You have always known it. You need only to be spurred.

So I ask you now to be as fair to yourself and to Jesus as you try to be with your students and your literary research. I will be thinking of you as you make decisions about what to do, and I hope you'll let me know what you find.

Yours,
Mark

April 28, 1977

Dear Mark,

I'm supposed to be cramming for an exam in transformational grammar. The book is in my lap, but my head is in the heavens, and trying to concentrate on phonemes seems completely impossible!

Are you familiar with the poems of T. S. Eliot? I think particularly of the line:

We shall not cease from exploration

And the end of all our exploring

Will be to arrive where we started

And know the place for the first time.

I've always ached to get to a place like that, for I seem to go around and around and around with no rhyme or reason. There's been enough energy for the journey, but no motivation to go. Now, though, the world's been turned upside-down.

Your last letter angered me a little (as you knew it would), but the remarks about my need to be a good scholar really hit home, and I decided to take them to heart. You are right—truth matters, whatever price has to be paid. And a great price has been paid, as I have discovered. But it was worth it.

You've been praying for me, haven't you? I know it. I have felt your presence with me so strongly. Would you consider this an answer to your prayers? It's an announcement from last Sunday's bulletin at University Presbyterian Church: "Hope Martin made a confession of faith to the Session at its last meeting. She will be baptized and admitted to the Lord's table during our service today.''

Me? Is this the *me* you meant? While I've been spitting in the Almighty's eye all these years, he's been waiting. He wants me; he's been wooing me. Armed with Freud and Bertrand Russell, I went forth to battle with him again, but once and for all came up against a force I could not break by the power of my will. Something began to work in me instead of me working on it. All the intellectual knots began to unravel. I began to see my dedicated apostasy as a mess of pottage while a banquet sufficient to fill all my hunger was waiting elsewhere.

How furious I used to get with you when you suggested that all my mental problems had spiritual roots! Of course I resisted the truth of that idea. Are all neurotics like me, refusing to accept their own natures, ignoring the thing that could heal them, kicking and screaming against the love of God while desperately substituting food or sex or money or ideas? None of it works. It never has and it never will. The raging hunger for understanding and acceptance can be satisfied with no earthly thing. Oh, Mark. I can't put metaphysics into words. He has found me now, this Jesus. The living, loving one. And I've thrown in my lot with him, and now I'm racing through the cosmos at a million miles a minute.

My coming to Michigan was no accident. He's been waiting for me here, waiting to trip me into his sweet net of love. After your challenge to me about going to church, I stepped into the one nearest to the dorm, just to prove you wrong. But I heard them talking about grace, not hellfire and brimstone. This forgiving, reconciling

Jesus was news to me. For as long as I can remember, I've been lugging around a heavy bag of self-hate and fear and guilt and tension. They told me Jesus, knowing all the horrible contents of that bag, had already picked it up and hurled it away. Why? I demanded to know. What was in it for Jesus? Nobody gets something for nothing.

Jesus has always been one of two things to me: an anemic face in a Sunday-school portrait or a condemning judge threatening to exile me to lakes of flame. I had honestly never realized that the cross was for me personally, and that Jesus would have suffered on Calvary even if I were the only person on earth. I resisted this challenge to my old ideas, for I've known so little love. But I did what every good scholar does—checked the text—and found my old theories refuted. There it was, over and over. "I love you, I *love* you, I love *you*." Suddenly it got under my skin, and my resistance started to melt.

Sometimes my students fear to use new words if they are not sure of the meaning. This happened to me with Jesus. But my confidence in him grew as my knowledge increased. Finally I spoke his name. "Jesus," I said. "Jesus, if you mean this, I want you. I want you so much."

It's hard for me to believe that anybody could want me, and I don't know much about giving and receiving love. But he took over. I heard people saying to me, "Hope, you look different... happy... pretty." *Me?* With the thick glasses and the zits and the fifty extra pounds? Could I be so transformed? Was I really reflecting the relief I felt in finding an anchor? I must have been, for my face looked different even to me. No longer did I have to produce, perform, get good grades to impress people. I only had to act the drama of my life for an audience of one, who was already pleased.

Mark, it's awesome. You are no longer just a doctor, but my brother. I can hardly comprehend something so mystical and strange. Now I have a therapist who understands me completely, who never runs out of energy, who is on call twenty-four hours a day. Under his nurturing care I feel myself opening up and discovering resources I never knew I had. Eliot writes of "A condition of complete simplicity/Costing not less than everything." That's what it feels like to be a Christian. Everything has to be re-examined in this new light, much old baggage cast away. But there is strength and motivation for the task.

When they poured the water over me in church that morning, my soul leaped up a thousand feet even as the floor beneath me seemed to turn to marshmallows. The organ swelled with "A Mighty Fortress Is Our God." As I left the church, a soft rain began to fall, as if God was putting a final touch on our covenant. And I knew that I had come home at last. I marvel and tremble at what lies ahead. Here I wait, a new baby in the body of Christ, held in hands that are going to mold me into all that I am capable of becoming.

Thank you for helping me to come to this place. Because of you, and others like you who pointed the way to this wondrous love, I can at last look at the name my parents gave me and know that it fits.

Love,
Hope

May 31, 1977

Dear Hope,

I have shared your letter with some friends, and they have become as excited as I am about your experiences as a Christian. Janice and I have wanted to show it also to some relatives who are having a difficult time understanding what it means to make the transition you have made from looking at religion intellectually to integrating it with the realities of life around us. For whatever part I played in helping this to happen to you, I am delighted. I only hope that your growth will continue for the rest of your life, and that God and Jesus will become more real to you as you mature.

Don't be afraid to ask questions as you grow. Yet be willing to admit answers that do not comfort you, that even confuse you and seem inconsistent. God's Spirit will guide you into all truth, though getting there may seem slow and laborious. Many times your spiritual walk will exhaust you, but remember that God is near at hand in those moments. I don't know what voice of confidence I can be for you in the months and years to come. But I want you to know that I am available and that I pray for you to know God's peace in the face of adversity, God's strength in time of weakness, and God's love when you see the lack of loveliness all around you.

What are you reading these days to keep tabs on your growth? C. S. Lewis is a great joy to me, and I also like to grapple with Brunner and Berkouwer, though you may find them a bit heavy at this point. You might also consider doing some writing of your own. I pray that someday your words will help people to understand more clearly the lives that they lead and to find joy in those lives. If this is the work Christ wants you to do, he will complete it in you as time passes. Meanwhile, rest assured that his watching eye is on you and his hand rests on your shoulder to encourage you at all times.

Blessings be with you!
Mark

August 1, 1977

Dear Mark,

Your last letter inspired me so. Even over the long distance that separates us, you continue to counsel me. Truly I have been recompensed with joy a hundred-fold since I came into the kingdom. If we Christians are the fingers of God doing his work on earth, consider yourself the indispensable thumb.

It's been a hectic summer for me. I'm enrolled in two seminars, am teaching three classes and have been tapped to direct the entire language-testing program in our Center. It seems incredible that less than a year ago I knew nothing of the English-as-a-second-language profession and that now duties seem to fall from the skies. I wonder where God is leading me through that. I do like the work more and more. My teaching gets better every day, I think. Certainly being in front of students every day is marvelous for building self-confidence. I don't have enough time to devote to library work, now that I'm drafting my thesis, but it doesn't bother me too much. When I study the Bible, I am amazed by how *active* the people are. Jesus took time for study and reflection, of course, but he came out of that meditation charged to heal and teach and preach. This leads me to wonder about the value of study-for-the-sake-of-study that one contends with so often in graduate school. Perhaps I enjoy teaching because it demands action and response to the needs of others in a very immediate and powerful way.

Undoubtedly you heard news of the flood two

weeks ago that devastated my hometown—the town where my parents still live. When I saw the evening news with its vivid pictures of the torrents ripping out roads and tearing up bridges, I got really frightened. All phone lines were out, and Red Cross reports were vague. It was two days before I got word that my family was safe, though all the topsoil was literally stripped off Dad's land by the rain and washed down the river. That spells the end of his business, though at least the house survived. I wonder how my father will be able to start over again at his age. What will that mean for all of us?

Water. That liquid symbol of salvation that rinsed my soul with life also baptized the land of western Pennsylvania with death and destruction. Many people died or lost all their possessions. The irony is that a dam didn't break this time, nor was there human error. There was simply a torrential onslaught of rain after a long dry spell, and the soil couldn't absorb the moisture. As a result, terrible loss and suffering. Why did God allow it? I know that's an ageless and worn question, but it's not a stupid question. This was senseless, a freak of nature, and God could have stopped it. But he didn't. And the innocent, like my dad, are the victims.

We must, I know, cling to the promise that God works everything together for good and that his grace is sufficient for us. I do not doubt these claims, Mark— but they're so often mouthed as platitudes that we neglect to grapple with their very profound implications. They demand from us a total, unwavering, almost inhuman level of trust. They rob us of our smugness and our easy certitudes. Of course it is all right to ask questions of God

—a God who won't stand up to questioning isn't worth believing in. But beyond a certain point questions are futile. It comes down to a matter of faith or faithlessness, and circumstances sometimes make it terribly, achingly hard to stand on the side of the faithful.

What a bawling infant I am in the knowledge of God. This rarefied academic air can stunt one's growth in him because it demands allegiance to so many other things. Day after day passes with me so wrapped up in my lesson planning and test proctoring and paper writing that I even forget to thank him for the roses and the zinnias, which are extraordinarily lovely on campus this summer. I don't appreciate enough the new friends he is bringing my way or the wonderful church I am part of or the young man that I have been spending some memorable time with. I need to be more grateful for these blessings, and to devote more time to praising and learning the ways of the Giver.

I hope to pop home for a few days when the term ends to check on things there. If I should happen to get in the general vicinity of Harrisville or Cedar Valley, I will give you a call. What a delight it would be to meet you as a fellow disciple! Thanks so much for your caring and prayers.

Peace,
Hope

September 15, 1977

Dear Hope,

I am sad that we didn't get a chance to be together when you came this way. It's so hard to make schedules coincide when the time is brief. We'll plan another reunion, and meanwhile I will continue to hear from you, won't I? Hearing of your experiences and knowing of your growth excites me. By now your fall term should be underway. How do you see the future shaping up as you begin your second year of graduate school? I'll pray that your work progresses smoothly and that you will find it stimulating.

Please be patient in your process of spiritual growth. You have a tendency, I think, to be impatient because you are not growing quickly enough. You reanalyze and reinterpret everything that happens to you. This hunger to know and grow will run into snags because there are so many interpretations of what Christian life means. I urge you to take the time to understand where all these interpretations come from instead of judging them hastily or condemning them out of hand. In many cases you will gain understanding more rapidly than others, because you are so ready for growth and have such an intellectual capacity for it.

Since we live in an ambiguous world, Christian people contradict themselves all the time. Try to accept the contradictions and guide others through them instead of setting yourself as the caustic adversary. Your gift of words is a terrifying gift because it can wound as well as heal. With God's help you may be able to use your gift to translate your spiritual experience into terms that bring nurture and beauty to others. This is the call of the teacher, isn't it? And the writer. One thing we lack today is people who do high-quality writing. Many claim to be Christians, many become popular, but the theoretical underpinnings of their work are often weak (popularized psychology is a good example). If you strive to be patient, Hope, you may be able to make a very significant contribution in the area of writing someday.

When you feel the need to be reminded of God's great love for you, read Psalm 103. For years I have been warmed and reassured by the words of this great poem. "As high as the heavens are above the earth, so great is His steadfast love toward those who fear him." Such words help us to stand on the side of the faithful through the most miserable experiences. I am glad, so very glad, that we both share in the bounty of that love. I am glad you are a Christian. Janice and I pray for you often. Share with me the areas where you feel the greatest need for support and encouragement, and I'll do my best to offer what I can.

Once again, I'm sorry we weren't able to meet, but know that my thoughts are often with you.

Your dear friend,
Mark

II
DARKNESS VISIBLE

No light, but rather darkness visible
Served only to discover sights of woe...

Milton/Paradise Lost 1. 63-64

November 21, 1977

Dear Mark,

Assume your best sagelike posture and answer a question for me. How do I love God back?

Caught in the spell of this bleak, black November, I have decided that I don't like God. For weeks I've been trying to convince myself that I had a false conversion, that apostasy suits me better than faith. Church bores me, devotions bore me, the pious platitudes of my brothers and sisters bore me. Reconciling myself to God doesn't seem worth it. I'm sinking, sinking. Only one thing buoys me up—the intellectual solidity of my belief. Deep inside, I know that I can't abandon truth.

But the agony of it! Oh, these impossible promises of God's, these incredible commands, these givens that are both sublime and ridiculous. I don't know what to do with this troublesome creed called Christianity. Who will rid me of it? My friends tell me they will pray for me in the dark hours through which I am now passing. I believe them, but the meaning and intent of their prayers cannot penetrate me. I am lost. I know that my friends mean well. But their good intentions can't fill my emptiness, and I find little comfort in the all-too-familiar clichés about pain bearing the fruit of righteousness.

The problem is not with God. It's with me. I'm unfit for him. I don't know how to love him. Part of me believes his pledges of eternal care and protection, but at my deepest core I'm as closed to him as if I were encased in iron. Cerebrally, I can accept it all—but what warmth is there in cerebral faith alone? I can accept that all my present turmoil has not come about because he wants to punish me or because I did anything wrong. Intellectually, I accept what Psalms and Job teach about his great unconditional love. But how do I make myself *feel* it? How do I feel it enough to respond as I should, to sing his praises in spite of my struggles? Help me, please help me to grasp this awful love of his for me.

Tell me, wise man in the east, how can I go down on my knees and thank God for my affliction? Affliction? Oh, Mark, I am sick. It's been six weeks since the first onslaught of pain. Without a single cent of health insurance, I've had to take myself to an ophthalmologist, a neurologist, an internist and two osteopaths. I've had an EEG and a CAT-scan and blood tests and x rays and all the rest, and still no one knows precisely why I hurt. It's my eyes. *Eyes.* This affliction threatens to prevent me from doing the only things I do well—reading, writing, researching. Why has God allowed this?

It started slowly. A bit of throbbing whenever I read. After all these years in school I've had enough experience with eyestrain to ignore such aching. But then the swelling and watering began. Then, excruciating comets of pain began to flash from the back of my head, shooting into my eyes and back again, doubling and darkening my vision. Something like a migraine, yet something all its own. Reading aggravates it to the point where I'm now having my assignments read to me by volunteers. What future do I have in the academic world with a handicap like this? I can't teach well because of the constant aches, and my library work and my thesis have gone straight to hell. All I can do is lie here, my eyes red and throbbing and itching. To top it off, the enthralling atheist friend with whom I have been spending some wonderful time has walked out on me because the sight of my suffering revolts him. He said, "I just can't stand you like this!" and disappeared. How can I believe that God has a place for me in his kingdom? If he does, why doesn't he take me there and give me peace? Surely he doesn't enjoy seeing me helplessly spaced out on Darvon. Why won't he let the doctors find out what it is so they can fix it?

I want to know how to reach out to a God who says he loves me in spite of all this. I want to know how to surrender all that this God wants. I would gladly give him my mind—that's the only good part of me anyway—and it's already his, lock, stock and barrel. But he wants my feelings and my thoughts and my afflicted body; he wants sovereignty over this muck and slime called me. How do I hand that over? What kind of a God would want such a thing? I don't know how to respond to a demand so all-encompassing. Does anyone? Do you? I can comprehend my atheist's kind of love—he likes me when I'm fine and fit, rejects me when I'm sick and scared. That's the kind of love that makes sense. Christ's doesn't.

You see, I accept what Christ did on the cross, and I'm glad he did it, but it would be so much easier to follow him if he coerced me or made conditions. Coercion is logical. But here's this God saying, "I love you. I want you to love me back and obey me to express your delight in me. Obey me freely because you want to, not because you have to." Who can cope with such awful freedom, Mark? How do I cope with a request like that when I am in so much pain? I'd rather have a set of black-and-white rules to follow to the letter on pain of death or hellfire. But no . . . this overwhelming love, this expansive passion of God for me just paralyzes me. Why won't he let me alone? How can he go on wanting me when I'm moaning and groaning and sinning against him? It terrifies me to think how he is waiting now for me to come and be reconciled. I don't want that responsibility. If he wants me, why do I have to go to him—why won't he come and just take me and demand that I love him?

Giving and expressing love is so hard for me. I want it desperately, but since I don't know how to respond to it, it always flees from me. I've gone back to see Sarah, the counselor I worked with last year. She is not a Christian and much of her therapy violates Christian teaching, but I need someone to talk to and the clinical atmosphere is so much less threatening than church and prayer. Do you hate me for saying that? I feel so guilty saying it, but my way to the Great Physician is blocked, and I can't see my way clear to him. If only I knew how to give myself to him totally. If only I would die. The pain would peacefully ebb away then, and there would be peace.

Yes, Mark, I know that wishing to die makes a travesty of the cross, but . . . But. Always *but*, or *yet*, or *still*, or *on the other hand*. Such conjunctions are yet another barrier between me and God. Every time I recognize a truth, I can so easily tack on a *but* or a *yet* to keep myself from having to change something. Sage, what can you say to me? Can you heal me? Can you say the words that will break down the walls I have built around me? I reach to you in desperation, I reach over miles and time, I reach for your hand as I once reached for it on a night when the world had collapsed. Do you remember how you came from the hospital to the dormitory where I was screaming and how surprised I was that you had come? I was frightened then by the evidence of your love, as I am now frightened by God's. Perhaps I am wrong to ask you to help me now—I feel guilty doing it—but my need is so big, and the light is so dim.

Hope

November 28, 1977

Dear Hope,
I love you!

Mark

P.S. More to follow.

December 4, 1977

Dear Hope,

Being a sage is new to me, but I'll try my best to impart some wisdom about what's happening to you right now. First of all, I really meant what I said in that short note to you last week. I didn't have time then to respond to all your questions, but I wanted you to be sure of my love and concern for you. Whether you believe it or not, I find a magnificent beauty in your struggle to grow and grapple with spiritual problems. Your openness to this growth frightens you because it leaves you so terribly vulnerable; you are not capable of deluding yourself. This is your beauty. Your difficulty stems from your trying so hard to understand what all of this means.

You sense yourself as being unable to love. Specifically, this difficulty comes from your inability to love your own parents. Do you remember going over this in our sessions? Well, God represents a kind of Supreme Parent. When the Parent says, "I love you," it demands a reaction. I mean *demands!* There is no way to get around this demand passively. Either you reject the love of God or you accept it—there is no middle ground. Thus we must, somehow, loosen ourselves up enough to be committed, one way or another, about the way we are going to live. I don't mean living a puritanical ethic based on negativism either; I'm talking about a thriving existence based on God's love. Love is serious and terrifying because it calls for such an all-or-nothing response. The family trains us for response to this love. If you feel that

44

your parents failed in loving, then reaching for God requires an even more intimidating leap of faith. For you have no precedent to assure you that you won't be cheated or hurt.

I'm not surprised that you find church and devotions boring. Spiritual growth, dear Hope, is not rooted in words that we read or creeds that we quote. It's rooted in our ability to share whatever resources we have in our personalities. I gain most in my spiritual life when I share what has been given to me. No, I don't mean a show-and-tell session or the giving of testimony. I mean really reaching into the lives of others and learning to be a trustworthy friend to them. Since you cannot do this right now, you feel that you are pulling away from God. Do you recall how Jesus asked Peter three separate times, "Peter, do you love me?" Each time Peter answered, "Yes." Jesus then concluded, "Feed my sheep." We cannot treat God's great love for us as a personal possession. It must be given. It's *intended* to be given. How and where and when to give it is a decision all of us make for ourselves.

When God told Jeremiah what to do, Jeremiah tried to keep it to himself. As a result, he felt the word of God like a burning fire shut up in his bones. He could not be silent because he was called to share the word. For you, Hope, the time has come for you to reach into the lives of other people. You will fling back at me that your present suffering renders you incapable, that you are too unsure of your faith. Aren't those just more barriers, more walls that you are building to shut out God? Aren't you trying to relieve yourself of the awful responsibility of living in his love?

45

I don't even pretend to understand the trouble with your vision. I only know that my guts ache inside out to think that you hurt and that you may possibly lose your ability to see in the years to come. Even thinking may be agony for you because of the pain. Be careful, though, not to rule out career hopes and dreams for the future. God is saying, "Hope, rest in me and I will help you take care of it." This gentle promise is so hard to cling to because it asks you to relinquish control, to adapt, to adjust, to use your gifts and resources in new, unfamiliar ways. And it's easy, so easy for me to quote that promise to you because I don't have any physical disorders that threaten my own position right now. Hope, I don't know why people suffer and die. Nor do I know why dear friends of mine have just suffered heart attacks and diabetes. I only know that it happens to them, that God cares for them, that I love them and that I love you. Jesus knew what it was to suffer. When you suffer, he therefore knows what you are going through and can empathize, not merely pity. But he can strengthen you only if you share the horror of your pain with others, as you reach with all the trust you can summon to the love that beckons you and give in to its firm protection.

What can I say about this atheist of yours? It's easy to be an atheist; you don't have to commit yourself to anything. Certainly an atheist need have no compassion for others who are in misery. Have you selected this man because he shares your own problems of being unable to reach out, to let go? He may be increasing your doubts right now because you are so weak and your need so great. I pray that you will hold to what you already know about atheism—it leads only to grief and meaningless-ness. Think rather of the Apostle Paul. He struggled and suffered all the time, but found such joy in it. He knew where he was going, what it was for and the peace brought by God's love. He knew this especially when he shared his knowledge and experience with everyone.

Your counselor Sarah may not grasp the one great assurance you need: that God always, always, *always* carries his own through every dark place. I don't fault you for returning to her, but be mindful of her limitations. As impossible as it may be for you to believe, this dreadful clamp on your ability to function and to give may turn out to be the greatest asset you will ever have . . . if you let it. I don't mean to sound heartless. I really believe that there may be a message in this for many people. Write a journal if you can these days. To the limits of your ability let others share the pain. It's such a fantastic opportunity for you to really confront the love that is waiting for you. So easy, isn't it, for me to tell you to press on when you're the one who has to live with it? No. It isn't easy. We are members of the same body, which means that your pain is also mine and that I do feel it with you.

Believe me, Hope, when I say that I have a deep well of concern for you. I'll pray that this cup passes from you soon and that till it does, God's will and purpose will be clear. Please keep me posted.

In the love of our Lord,
Mark

December 15, 1977

Dear Mark,

Thanks for lavishing so much time on your reply to my yell for help. In some ways it was a pretty cold-blooded response—but perhaps that is what I need at this point. Still, how can I think of sharing the intensity of this pain, which grows more acute every day? I am so grateful that you care about me, Mark, and wish I could do what you say is necessary. You are right. I have put up a lot of defenses against him, but there's little energy to devote to reconciliation when I can think of nothing but the hurt.

Keep a journal? I feel like I've got two water-filled balloons ready to burst inside my head. How can I think of writing when a line of fine print teases the swollen surface of my eyes like a sword? A friend is writing this letter as I dictate. It's the first time in my life that I've had to ask someone to write for me, and I feel little excitement at requesting someone else to do what is so fundamental to my being. You quoted Scripture to me. I want to quote some back at you: "The eye is the lamp of the body. So if your eye is not sound, your whole body will be full of darkness. If then the light in you is darkness, how great is the darkness!"

That was sarcastic and unfair. I'm sorry. I have no beauty in me these days. The panic within me grows and grows as I consider the postponed reading and the untouched research. Every medical "breakthrough" leads to another problem, and I am trotted off to yet another

48

specialist. The doctor count is now at eleven. The bills are spiraling. I don't know where on earth the money is going to come from.

Do you know much about osteopathic medicine? It's new to me, but apparently it's been well accepted here in Michigan for years. The doctor now in charge of my case is a D.O. who is studying a new therapy called "cranial manipulation." It seems that osteopaths believe that most disease stems from muscle deterioration, and they think they can restore "structural integrity" to muscles through massage. The doctor asked how I would feel about having his new therapy tried on me, and I agreed since I'm tired of being drugged all the time. For the past month I've gone to his office four times a week. In the course of the treatment he has discovered that all the muscles of my head and face are out of whack. The jaws and teeth and eyes interfere with each other, and I should have my entire face rebuilt when there's enough money and time. Meanwhile, he massages and twists and squeezes and stretches the muscles of my head, my neck—even the inside of my mouth. It does assuage the pain—temporarily. For about an hour afterwards I feel marvelous; then the throbbing comes back and seems more acute because of the brief respite.

The strangest part of it is the doctor's constant touch. At first his warm, firm hands frightened me so much. I have not been touched very much in my life. I don't know how to react. But now I wonder if part of the value of osteopathic healing comes from the reassuring feel of human hands laid on me. The hands somehow affirm my own worth. Does that make sense? If only Jesus could touch me, it would be so much easier to reach to him. Why has he made himself so distant, so spiritual, when I need his holy fingers to envelop me and hold me close?

So as I lie there, I waste my energy on anger. Why must I plod, dizzy with pain and fatigue, through bitterly snowy afternoons across the campus, to lie motionless while this muscle master sweats over me trying so hard to heal what God could fix in a minute? Why are other people normal when I am a maze of bad connections, a warped torture of misplaced parts? Why does it hurt when I look into the light? I can cope in part by thinking metaphorically. I don't much like to look on the piercing brilliance of God because of what it reveals about me. So perhaps my eyes hurt now because they are tired of looking. I don't want to face the fact that I am broken, sinful, defiant.

I'm just exhausted, Mark, and rambling. I need to conserve every ounce of energy, for I plan to make a brief trip home to my folks tomorrow and that's a long way to travel. I really don't want to travel so far, but I don't want to spend Christmas in a dorm either. Please pray for me. I'll write after the new year.

Hope

December 21, 1977

Dear Hope,

The most blessed Christmas to you. It's the season for miracles. I am with you in prayer and God is near.

Love,
Mark

January 4, 1978

Dear Mark,

The snow is so light and gentle tonight that I think a great goose pillow has burst in heaven and drifted to earth. (Perhaps the angels are having a party.) The new year has broken, and so far there is nothing tempestuous about it. It's quiet, soft and anticipatory—as I am. I am safely back at school after a most revealing holiday, and I feel quiet too. Maybe the approach of Epiphany gives me the impression that God is circling around me very close and that he's about to show me how much he loves me... though I don't know how yet.

The two weeks in Pennsylvania were punctuated with the most agonizing physical suffering to date. I speculate that the sudden interruption of my regular massage schedule may have triggered the stunning reaction. My eyes swelled and ran. My face was an indescribable throbbing frenzy. There was no respite. It settled on me almost as soon as I got there and would not go away. I lost over ten pounds because I could keep nothing down, not even water, and I had to be carried everywhere for I simply had no strength left. I lay on the couch unable to do anything but groan. How awful it is to be incapacitated—and what a potent reminder of our fallen nature! Never before have I so appreciated what Adam's wholesomeness of body must have been like, and never have I felt myself living out his curse so vividly.

At times I would think about the creed I so often intone: *I believe in the resurrection of the body.* O God, I prayed, take me now, let me come home and be healed. But he didn't take me. So I continued on my earthly progress and went to my parents' doctor for an opinion. He said he wouldn't treat me "because you're under the care of an osteopath and they're all quacks." He did give me more Darvon, which I couldn't swallow. I returned home and lay in the shadow of the Christmas tree, gazing at the star which crowned it and wondering why God had abandoned me.

But it was Christmas. The season for miracles, you called it in your Christmas card. Yes, Bethlehem certainly demonstrates conclusively that nothing is impossible.

Two days before Christmas, I felt I could no longer go on in such agony. "Mother!" I screamed. When she came running, I said, "Call your minister. Call your deacons! I've got to have more than painkillers now—call them!"

Very soon the minister was shaking snow from his boots, and he knelt at my side, a vial of oil in his hand. He and the assisting deacon read from James, placed their hands on my head and prayed as the oil was poured over my head. They prayed especially that my faith would be strengthened; it was a very moving and holy moment. Until then I had not known much about the ceremony of anointing. A slow, easy peace came to me as I contemplated the great healing that would follow.

Next morning, shattering disappointment swept me when I realized that I felt as rotten as ever. Unfair! I cried to God. If you won't heal me, God, damn you, let me die!

But I had yet to see that a God who could make Christ could make anything happen. A seldom-seen uncle of mine popped in for a holiday visit later on that day. When he saw me, he got on the phone to a man that he skis with—one of the best internists in the state. The doctor agreed to see me as a favor to my uncle. And my uncle handed me a hundred dollars to pay the bill with.

The internist looked me over, suggested that I needed an endocrinological work-up and gave me a little speckled pill which I started taking right away. Within a day I could sit up and eat. Frankly, Mark, that was not the kind of healing I expected from God. I wanted at least a thunderbolt or an avenging angel or an apocalyptic renewal that I could write a book about. I did not want to be told that I was still ill and that a long road lay ahead. But as I sit here and type this letter, I realize that I am functional. He did not abandon me. Working through the medical profession, he *has* healed me, partially. Two weeks ago I wanted to die. Now I feel like living, and that proves how faithful God is.

Count your blessings, Hope. That's what I have learned in the recent days. Through the doctor and the pill and the new advice, grace has been liberally bestowed on me. Throughout my sickness, I have prayed (because it seemed like the proper thing to pray) that God would do whatever he needed to do to draw me closer to him. Is this thorn in my flesh his way of doing that? Is that the only way he can penetrate my resistant and stubborn hide? Is that what you were trying to tell me in your last letter?

A few weeks ago I wrote a wistful little poem:
Why can't doctors be like gods

And guarantee, despite the odds,
Salvation from a life of pain?
O please let me be born again!

When will my rebirth come? Will I never be well until God is finished instructing me in his ways? In the subject of his love I am such a slow and undisciplined student that I may suffer for years. Yet I feel he is near, waiting.

Does God owe me health? No, that's absurd. He doesn't owe me anything. My life itself is evidence of his great grace. On top of that grace are my work, my students, the fascinating set of individuals he has brought into my life. Somebody told me yesterday, "Hope, you have the most interesting collection of friends I've ever seen!" On top of that, I enjoy my research and know that I am honing my verbal and analytical gifts. My boss at the Center thinks I am creative and dedicated; my major professor says I'm the best student to come along in years. So what am I complaining about? How dare I gripe! I am ashamed that I casually demand from God more than I even deserve to think about. My life already overflows with his generosity. How dare I curse God for working out his purpose in me? I am his.

As I ache and have yet another blood test and still another humiliating disrobing for every new doctor, it's hard to count blessings. But I do have many—not only food, shelter, comforts, people, a fine education, a sense of community with others in the body of Christ, but also mountains, flowers, Milton's poems, El Greco's paintings and Vivaldi's choruses. I have already been so abundantly enriched. Why can't I be content instead of always filling out my demand sheet?

Nothing is out of his hands. I still believe this in my head, and it may sooner or later seep into my heart.

Thank you, dear Mark, for all that you have been and are to me.

Love,
Hope

February 3, 1978

Dear Mark,

Under the knife we go, we go. On the 13th. They say it's time for some scissors-and-glue work.

After I last wrote to you, the pain resurged. I was relieved of teaching duty for the term, put on new medication and trotted off to two more specialists. What they have decided is so anticlimactic that I could almost laugh if I weren't hurting so much. The endocrinologist said my thyroid is in mint condition; there are no tumors, no growths, no malignant molecules anywhere inside of me. It's just the muscles. The muscles have been in the wrong place since I was born but waited this long to complain. A periodontist, of all people, summed it up in terms that made sense: "You have a number of congenital deformities in your eyes and mouth which haven't bothered you for years. But now you are in a high-stress environment that weakens your powers of resistance, so things like this have a way of surfacing. The massage treatment might work if you give it five years, but surgery would accomplish the same thing much more quickly."

So that's it. I feel embarrassed that I don't have a glamorous disease with a mile-long Latin name. Muscles ... it's so simple. Yet the thought of someone cutting into my eyes to move muscles around is anything but simple. I am afraid. Even though it will make me feel better, I am afraid. Please pray for me this next week!

Hope

February 9, 1978

Mark!

Your call really hit me like a bolt from the blue. I'm so embarrassed that I didn't recognize your voice! I guess I've gotten so used to communicating with you on paper that your deep bass doesn't register as much as your penmanship.

Your concern and the invitation to visit you and Janice and the boys when it's over warmed me in the midst of this winter. And thank you so much for telling me that there was nothing wrong with being petrified. People have been complimenting me on how controlled, rational and collected I seemed about the approaching surgery. Deep down I've been so scared, but haven't wanted to show my fear. After you called and we had talked about it, I went to bed and dreamed the most vivid dream about being operated on, complete with blood and slipped scalpels and assorted atrocities.

I woke up screaming and vomited for ten minutes. Then I went to sleep again and awoke more rested and relaxed than I had in two weeks. The loving cadences of your voice reminded me that it was okay to let go and to show how I felt. Thanks.

As soon as I'm functional after the surgery, I will write and fill you in. I hope we can get together next month. But we will be meeting in prayer before then!

Love,
Hope

February 27, 1978

Dear Mark,

I've been swimming, swimming on a sea of love and grace from the moment I woke up in the recovery room. Thank you for all your prayers; the energy around me could have come from no other source. Though I've not been able to pray for myself, my needs have been provided for at every turn. When these tremendous waves of love keep washing over me, it is harder and harder for me to believe in my own unlovability.

Waking up and finding myself unable to see because of the bandages really put me into a tailspin, even though I had been prepared for it. Worse, I felt like the devil himself was pulling on my eyes with red-hot pincers. I wish I could say I was heroic, but I wasn't. I screamed constantly. And that sodium pentathol took *so* long to wear off. Now I know what it feels like to be *really* drugged. But apparently there was a lot of traffic in my room even while I was unconscious. The women in my Bible study group kept a vigil. People from the Center—all pagans and apostates—kept the telephone lines burning and filled my room with Valentines and plants. One of them gave me two hundred dollars to help pay the surgeon. I later received the most affirming gift from some comrades in the English department: a gift certificate to a bookstore. They have faith that I will be reading soon with all my old vigor.

Through it all, my "proxy" parents stood by me. The elder who baptized me and his wife passed the vomit pans and the bedpans, took me into their home for my convalescence, fed me royally, pampered me like a princess and cheerfully helped me with impossible chores like bathing and hair washing. Emma even did the dreadful eye-washes. She took off the bandages, put in the special drops and cleaned all the sticky matter from my lids and lashes. I look so absolutely hideous that I thought she would retch from the sight of me—but she just kept smiling. Now that the bandages are off for good, what the world sees is blood-red where the white should be, surrounded by pink-blue swelling. Yuck! Little pieces of thread from the sutures keep working their way out.

Yet even that has been cause for affirmation. The man who walked out on me last November because he couldn't endure my suffering dropped in a few days ago and studied my face. "There's a thread in your eye," he said wonderingly. "Do you have tweezers?" So I got them, and he plucked it out, ever so gently. I *never* thought he would be able to do anything like that, and truly I thank God!

What all this great outpouring demonstrates to me is the truth of an old bromide: your works cannot redeem you. A few years ago I would have smirked in disbelief if my academic adviser had told me, "We know you can't perform right now and that's okay." I would have hooted if my friends had said, "We know you can't do anything for us right now, but we can do something for you and that's okay." I'm so conditioned to having to *do* things to win acceptance and respect. But now when I have hit bottom, everyone from the dean to the church janitor has come through for me, and they have empowered me to reciprocate in kind. This love has made me *want* to love back to show my gratitude and express my delight, and to glorify in everything him who has made this magnificent demonstration of good will so present to me.

And some new doors have opened for me as a result of the pain. After five-and-a-half years of dorm life, I'm going to move into a house with two women from the church. They made the offer because they felt they could look after me until I was completely well, because they know how financially pressed I am, and because they thought it would be good for all of us to try communal living. I hope that we all learn and mature from it. By the way, I also got accepted to pursue doctoral studies at the University of Pennsylvania, so a decision about what to do next fall is imminent. If my health continues to mend well, I will try to visit Philadelphia over spring break to check out the school. If I manage to get that near, I will stop up to see you. I hunger to see you again and to meet Janice and your sons. These links with our Christian brothers and sisters are so vital. Most of the Christians I know seem so different from me at first glance. We seem to have nothing in common, but I soon discover that the more I peel from their surface, the richer and sweeter they become. Every day in the kingdom of God is Christmas, with a wealth of packages to be opened and savored.

That was a mixed metaphor—how revolting! I'm gushing, aren't I? I'm at such a peak that I'm bubbling all over the place. I've been exalted right off the operating table. Somebody recently introduced me to Handel's *Israel in Egypt.* Music more than anything else helps me to grasp God's grandeur, and throughout my ordeal I have listened to that swelling baroque chorus erupt into "Thy right hand, O Lord, is become glorious in power!" It has reminded me that there is a force in this cosmos bigger and better than I who has me in his care, and I can say a hearty *Amen!*

When my plans firm up, I will be in touch. Right now, I'm going to close because the double vision still plagues me a bit. It has been a joy to be able to say these things to you. Thank you for your care and the comfort it has given me.

Love,
Hope

March 5, 1978

Dear Hope,

Praise God! You made it through the worst. Janice and I have been praying steadily for you, especially that your friends would be near at hand to help support you through this. Our prayers have been more than abundantly answered. What a confirmation this is for us, as well as for you!

What is it about you, Hope, that whenever I read your letters, I find my heart full of joy and my eyes close to tears? I keep coming back to the word *beauty*, for your beauty is indescribable. Whether it stems from your spiritual youthfulness, your perceptions, your verbal gifts—I do not know where it comes from, but it is special to me. I find that I want to share your letters with almost everyone I come in contact with, because what you write is so vibrant. Please don't consider that a standard to maintain, but just an expression of my thanks for allowing your life to be open to me.

We will pray about the decision you must make about graduate school in the fall. Our home is open to you whenever you pass this way—but be mindful of your physical needs and don't feel pressed to do anything until you are more fully recovered. If you're lonely and need someone to talk with, please call me collect and let me know what is troubling you. I will be glad to share whatever I have to offer.

The intimacy that people experience when they are members of the kingdom of God is truly beyond words.

As your letter attests, you've begun to taste some of the fruits of the Spirit and the love he gives through the people who have aided you lately. Now that you have tasted, your hunger will increase, and I thank God that this has happened to you at this point in your development. At last you are beginning to believe in your own lovability, something you have always undervalued (even dismissed) as part of yourself. A while ago, you cried out to me that there appeared to be no reason for your suffering, but now that I have your most recent letter, I see a glimmer of an answer. Do you? If you do, I'm delighted!

If your budding awareness of love causes you to mix metaphors, it doesn't bother me in the least!

So you find in Handel a source of strength and encouragement. I also find his music a profound comfort. The oratorios proclaim that all history is in God's hands and that all history will be triumphant in his actions. I can rest in that. It reminds me to do my part, but assures me that I don't have to do everything myself. Being in the family of God allows me to be nurtured when I am down, to be nurturing when I'm up. For now, it's important for you to be nurtured. You have missed a lot of this because of your parents' undemonstrative natures—they never touched you, showed an interest in your activities or spoke of their love. I am glad, so very glad, that you are now receiving nurture in such a dynamic way.

We will continue to pray for your recovery and that God will minister to you. His peace be with you.

With much love,
Mark

III
BREATH AGAINST
THE WIND

... prayer against his absolute decree
No more avails than breath against the wind,
Blown stifling back on him that breathes it forth...

Milton/Paradise Lost 11. 311-313

May 5, 1978

Dear Mark,

Naturally, I decided to stay here in Michigan to do my Ph.D. work. When I began to consider what it would mean to uproot myself, to make new friends, to find a new church and learn to navigate within a new academic bureaucracy, my feet got colder and colder. Perhaps I have taken the coward's way out. But now that I have accustomed myself to the decision, I am actually looking forward to the work. I'm going to continue to concentrate in eighteenth-century studies—obscurity of all obscurities!—which probably appeals to me because no one else will touch it these days. There's an excellent professor here to work with. The honest part of me admits, however, that I made the decision to stay not for professors or churches but because of Daniel's presence. I guess I have mentioned him in passing. I really love him quite hopelessly, but I won't bore you with the traumas of *that* relationship.

Before I begin doctoral study, I simply must do something about my living situation. This group-house stuff has been a jolt, considering what high hopes I had for it. When I read the Bible, I get the impression that Jesus calls us to some form of communal sharing and a lot of give-and-take, but then he didn't have housemates. If he had, I wonder if he could have endured them! Mine drive me nuts. Sometimes I find it impossible to compromise, especially when Denise is perennially late and Margaret leaves her plants in the bathtub. On the other hand, my insistence on meticulousness grates on them. I can't help it—I hate filth. I get angry with them for not doing their share of the chores, while they claim that my standards are too high and that I have to be more flexible. Theoretically, three Christian women ought to be able to work things out or to pray through them, but our human sides usually prevail when we try to talk things through rationally. The constant hassles consume too much time and energy. So I'll be moving into my own apartment next month, one closer to campus and to Daniel. I'd rather pay more rent than find somebody else's dirty underwear in the bathroom sink.

Going back to the hectic pace of a full schedule after a term of doing nothing has not been easy, and I feel drained most of the time. I'm teaching one delightful class, but the other is slow and unmotivated, which in turn unmotivates me. The seminars I've enrolled in are quite demanding, especially the one in colonial American literature. That one is becoming an exercise in faith-testing. When I see the extremes to which doctrinaire Calvinism was taken, I begin to worry about the foundation my faith is built on and where I stand. On top of Cotton Mather and Jonathan Edwards, I've been subjected to my pastor's latest series of sermons on the history of the Reformed faith. Last week, after his particularly cold-blooded exposition on predestination, I felt the stirrings of real revolt within. Predestination seems to me utterly irrelevant. To expand my horizons, I've begun to attend a Roman Catholic service on Wednesdays and an Orthodox mass on Saturday. It helps me to see beyond the narrow Calvinistic vista.

God is so big, and we are so limited. Any system

that claims to be the only true way frightens me. I find myself refreshed by radical people because they dare to challenge so many of the old sacred cows. Don't you sometimes think that Protestantism in general lays too heavy a stress on personal salvation and on the impending judgment? Of course those things are important, but so is justice on earth. Jesus was so active, so giving, so life-affirming. We have to be here for more than just conversion, self-denial and waiting to be ushered into the sweet by-and-by. If we are not engaged in building the kingdom of God right here and right now, then it all seems pointless. I just can't buy the idea that earthly life is a mere preliminary judging to weed out the sheep from the goats . . . or the elect from the damned.

Do I raise these intellectual objections to rationalize away the emptiness I feel, the tension within me because Margaret and Denise are driving me crazy and Daniel and I are at odds again? What happened to that marvelous outpouring of only a few months ago, the tremendous exaltation I felt? Why do I vacillate so much in my Christian life? After two years, I ought to have stabilized, but I just keep going from hot to cold all the time. One day I'm rejoicing; the next, cursing.

Recently the staff associate at my church accused me of—guess what!—building walls around myself and raising objections that can't be answered so that I'll have excuses not to be more active in church. I am so mad at her, Mark; I just can't forgive her. She insisted that anyone who had been as blessed as I have, *had* to give back. You've said the same thing, but you're not so brutal. She said I had to turn off my mind for a while and get to work on my detachment from many in my church family, and I would have to change the withdrawn, reticent attitude that so many people mistake for intellectual snobbery. She said that God demands that we do what is uncomfortable, because comfort always takes a backseat to obedience. "What is obedience?" I challenged her.

"Shake hands. Knock on doors. Take evangelism training and share the good news," she shot back. "You must *prove* that you have the Spirit of the living God within you."

Well, well, well. Tell me, Mark, about this God who requires that his grace work in opposition to the laws of psychology. I am what I am. If he insists that I do what I know I cannot do, then I want no part of him. Personal confrontation is not my style—I'm no evangelist and I'm no missionary. My own faith journey has not been of typical evangelical ilk. True, God showered his grace on me during my illness, but I thought it was grace given *freely*. Does God now say "Give back what I gave you"? Do I have to teach Sunday school or win souls because he healed me? That makes me mad! I did not realize his grace was conditional!

I wish he would let me alone. I wish all of them would let me alone. I have so many things I need to do, and God is forever in the way. I am tired of friends and roommates who constantly confront me about whether I am living in the will of God. It's like I have several pairs of critical eyes focused on my most personal and private concerns, scrutinizing them for error. If every word and deed is not pure and true, I'm sure to hear about it. That's the biggest trouble with roommates—they see everything and don't hesitate to tell you to shape up. The Inquisition is alive and well in Michigan.

Sure, I'd like to commit a few sins. But even without the eagle eyes of my roommates and the staff associate, God's hold on me is so strong that I can't do anything—except feel guilty about wanting to sin! Why do we always feel guilt? Go ahead—tell me that guilt is the human condition and Jesus came to relieve us of it. I believe you. But I will turn around and tell you that I've borne the crippling destruction of guilt about almost everything since I was a tiny child, and borne it with the most aching vividness. I'm tired of it. I'm tired of being told I'm a backslider because I don't whip myself into having daily quiet times, because I spurn evangelism training, because I prefer to spend more time with Dan than with my Bible study group. Frankly, Dan needs me more than the church does.

Wow. I sure harangue you a lot, don't I, Marcus? I call you my friend, and all I seem to do is gripe. I guess I have an impression of you as one who makes a living at curing guilt, so you're bound to understand my trials more than the average pew-sitter. I pray that you can read between the lines of my harangue and see the reverence I have for you. How are you these days?

Yours,
Hope

June 1, 1978

Dear Hope,

A lot of time has passed since I received your letter, including a week at a convention. When I got back, I found myself swamped with mail and am just now getting my hands on a lot of the correspondence I was aching to answer right away. Because I like to answer letters like yours immediately, I find myself angry and frustrated when things in the hospital have to take priority. Please don't get the impression that I am putting you aside. It just isn't true. The questions that you have raised concern me—perhaps *fascinate* is a better word. You may wince at that and wonder if I too am treating you cold-bloodedly. I don't think that I am, Hope. Your problems just get me excited!

You say that the Puritans have chilled you. When I read Calvin, I get the impression that the man was grappling with some very difficult times in Geneva. And those times are reflected to some degree in the theology that he developed. Any theology, I think, must be couched first of all in the cultural context in which it was written. The ability to abstract or to interpret comes only from a thorough grip of the foundations from which the theologian originally spoke. In my experience, many Christians, including some with rather strong Calvinistic tendencies, have great difficulty integrating Christianity with psychology; they tend to forget that all truth is God's truth. For this reason, I enjoy reading Carl Jung. Surely you have stumbled across Jung in your literary work. His book

71

Modern Man in Search of a Soul has helped me tremendously since I first read it in college. Do look it up.

So you revolt and go to Mass. That's fine. Did you think I would be shocked? When I was in Chicago recently, I too attended Mass. There was no meat to chew on in the homily, but then real confrontation with Christian life and ideas seldom flows from any pulpit these days, regardless of denomination!

Like you, I believe that God is big and unlimited. I agree that any system claiming to be absolute has many rejecting elements in it. The world in which we live is not black and white. I think God intentionally left us with ambiguity to test the first and second great commandments. Ambiguity forces us back to the reality that the primary ethic of life is "love one another." Love. It always comes back to that. About a decade ago I gave up the concept of the impending apocalypse as something beyond my comprehension that had little relevance for my daily living. I did not, however, throw out the baby with the bathwater. My task remains to love God, to enjoy him and to live with his creatures in love forever.

Love. Jesus affirms life because he is loving. God gives new understanding and revelations throughout history because of his great love for us. The natural world also mirrors this love. Watching a child be born attests to it. As I look at my sons and see them grow, develop and acquire skills step by step, I am enthralled, amazed at the things they are able to put together. To see them begin to struggle with ethical and moral questions awes me, especially as they move into knowledge of the great love that sustains them. Likewise, I am awed with the learning process of young Christians like you as you try to make your lives more meaningful. This is a life-affirming act, and you are following your Savior in it.

I do not accept the idea that we are called to denial. Denial for the sake of discipline can be helpful, but denial for the sake of piety is pharisaical. Are you sure which one of these your roommates and your church staff worker are hinting at in their criticisms of you? Do they really mean for you to do distasteful things for the sake of appearance—or are they trying to remind you to respond to love with love? Have you asked yourself honestly what shortcomings in you lead them to make their comments?

I am not tormenting you. But I do see that you grow so rapidly intellectually that you can easily put aside personal and social experiences as things of lesser importance. I can see you hiding behind books to avoid risking meeting other people. You did that at Harrisville College, and that's what drove you to my office in the first place. As I have said before, this is the time for you to use your gifts to glorify and honor God's love for you. It will be hell for you at first, but remember, you are doing it to become more free, not more constrained.

You do see, don't you? Lose yourself, abandon yourself in his love, Hope, even when it terrifies you. You have much more to offer socially than you believe you do. If for one year you keep reaching out to people with your being the assertive one, you will be astonished at the returns. Don't let the old fears of rejection hamper you. People *are* going to like you, but you will never conquer your old ideas and impressions of yourself until you take those first faltering steps of reaching out.

I don't know what to say about this idea you throw at me about God requiring his grace to work in opposition to the laws of psychology. Psychology doesn't have any laws. People who say that it does don't know what they're talking about. I have an intense affection for psychology, but also a keen awareness of its limits. Psychologists have turned religion into a subject for study, instead of viewing it as a force that has meaning for their lives. You seem to think some facets of your personality are not subject to the all-consuming love of God. That is not true. Psychology has not determined that you be what you are. *You* determine that.

You may then ask me, "If *I* determine what I am, why do I feel so much guilt?" Do you recall one of the great dictums of theology, *non posse non peccare?* This harks back to our friend Martin Luther and means "not able not to sin." Thus we feel guilt. You say that guilt is destructive (and it can be), but the absence of guilt is even more destructive. A person who never feels guilt has a sociopathic personality; he has no close relationships with anyone. Guilt guides us as we try to determine where our lives are going. The Holy Spirit's task is to guide us into right living, and he uses guilt to point out erroneous paths. Do you feel guilt now because you know you are in error? What about this man you are spending time with? A bit of guilt can help you to decide if that's the right thing to be doing.

You are not alone in your struggle with guilt. I too would readily choose to run away from God rather than walk toward him. I too would push someone away more quickly than I would draw him to me. Guilt directs me back to the proper path. When I draw close to God and feel that my thoughts are aligned with his, then the whole issue of guilt becomes insignificant. We are free from guilt when we focus on love. To put it another way, when we love, we act according to the will of God. As a result guilt disappears. Your prayer and devotional time is between you and God. No one has the right to criticize you. But if you are feeling guilt about it, you need to re-examine your time schedule to see if you are indeed giving God enough of your day.

I think you must seriously consider now how God wants to use your many talents and assets. Your letters indicate that you can no longer put this off. You are not satisfied, and will not be until you let God's will be done in you. Let me say, though, that I look forward very much to hearing from you and am glad you turn to me. I hope that I can continue to serve as your counselor for as long as I live. Rest assured that the struggles of the present time are going to bear fruit. Don't frustrate your brain, and give your heart some rest. Wait patiently beside the still waters—and be sure of the Shepherd's great love for you.

With much love and concern,
Mark

June 24, 1978

Mark!!!!

I am in the tropics! My first travel abroad! Right out of the blue, the university decided to send me over here as a consultant to administer an English-testing program. I had exactly ten days to get a passport and pack my bags! I feel like I've been hit by a bolt of lightning. Here I am in a place I never even dreamed of seeing!

Will write in detail when I return!

Love,
Hope

Holiday Inn
Manila, Philippines

July 13, 1978

Dear Mark,

Now that I'm back on the ground, I'm still trying to believe that I had such a wonderful adventure, halfway around the world. It came as a complete surprise to me; the director of the Center called me into his office one day and said, "How would you like to give English tests in Manila next week?" A group of nurses there who wanted to emigrate needed to be certified in English proficiency. So I was nominated, and the university paid for everything —plane fare, hotel, meals, sightseeing, plus my salary (would you believe a hundred dollars a *day?*). When I close my eyes, I can still see before me the shimmering blue water of Manila Bay, the palms waving languidly in the steamy heat rising from Roxas Boulevard. The people, so delicate and dark and high-spirited, completely charmed me. On my way home, I spent hours in ports that sound like the stuff dreams are made of—Seoul, Guam, Honolulu.

Wow! It's hard to come back to earth. I hunger now to see other sights, to travel to the four corners. Michigan seems so . . . ordinary.

Thank you so much for your last fine letter. I've read it several times, so that it will penetrate. You are right. What an arduous thing it is to live a genuine Christian life! Your words make it sound easy, but it never is, as we both know.

Specifically, I have been thinking of some of the sights I saw in Asia, the deprivation and need that even my calloused Western eyes could spot. I stayed in a luxurious hotel, my room filled with flowers and baskets of mangoes. I had a chauffeur; I was wined and dined. But I could not help seeing children whose skin clung to their bones and the most unspeakable filth and squalor. I saw all this, of course, from inside my air-conditioned car on my way to yet another fancy restaurant. The ethics that I profess kept coming into my mind. Likewise, I type this as I sit in my lovely new apartment with its thick yellow shag carpeting and its terrace and its well-stocked kitchen. Do I mock God when I live in such a place? Is it sin to have (and want) all this for myself? Or is the real sin in obliviousness to the blessings I have received?

When it comes right down to the facts, how much of my faith is lip service? If I were truly sincere, I'd be off planting potatoes for some starving aborigines. I'd give up *things*. But no, I'm a slave to the bourgeois. The stereo? No, I can't give that up; I just have to have music. The clothes? But I teach every day, and I have to look my best. The food? But, Lord, I love to entertain and must put out a nice spread for my guests . . . and so the list goes on. The worst of it is that I like my lifestyle. I don't want to change, nor do I want to be paralyzed with guilt just because I have drinkable water and a bathtub. Still, so many of the sights that I saw over there force me to ask these questions. You might reply that it's possible to be a middle-class Christian. Perhaps it is. But how do we strike a balance between the sacrificing, sharing example of Christ and the conditioning and brainwashing of a culture that screams instant gratification of every desire?

Cultural brainwashing on top of original sin

makes a potent concoction indeed. We are inclined to do evil by our very nature, and then our culture sanctions the evil we wish to do! Greed is sanctioned. "You deserve a break today... nothing's too good for you... pamper yourself." Greed and overconsumption and me-first-ism are praised from the airwaves and hailed from the billboards. Worse, this conditioning is not confined, by any means, to the merely materialistic aspect of life. I've been thinking a great deal lately about how sex comes into all of this and what God intends sex to be.

How do you strike a balance between Christian sexual ethics and the easy-going notions of the age? Or must it be one or the other? How can you remain oblivious to or unaffected by the deluge of sex that flows at you from every side in this country? I speak personally now. I'm 24, I live alone, and I function in a university environment where there are lots of interesting people my age with exceedingly liberal ideas. The whole immediate world has got its clothes off, and there I am in my chastity belt, waiting for the Lord to drop a husband like manna from the heavens.

Shall I turn to the church for support? No, the church is part of the problem. It exalts the wedded state, singing hosannas to monogamy at every opportunity. Since we are a university church drawing most of our congregation from the graduate and undergraduate population, we cannot ignore the issue. But we do it within the strictest confines. Students are perennially—what's a delicate word?—hot, and the heat has one remedy: find a mate and settle down. Last year alone, we had twenty engagements among members of our church. For those of us still unclaimed, the powers-that-be plan a battery of social events called "mixers" or "grad student and singles evenings" or "ice cream socials"—all geared toward the mating of the geese and the ganders. They'd be hysterically funny if they weren't so awkward. All the women have glints in their eyes, and the guys have that lean and hungry look. Eventually this proximity is supposed to breed fondness. There's yet another wedding, and we hear another sermon about the sanctity of the marriage bed and the delights of producing little Presbyterians. Do we get any savvy advice about what to do if the Almighty does not act on mixer night? No. We get speeches about discipline, about jogging and morning swims, about victory in Christ and waiting, waiting, waiting.

Now I don't have a lot of illusions about marriage. At least sixty per cent of the people I work with have been divorced at least once, and I have the example of my sister and brother-in-law as a mismatched pair at each other's throats. Of course some marriages work beautifully; you and Janice seemed to have managed it. But to rush into marriage as a panacea for sexual frustration strikes me as the pinnacle of idiocy. On the other hand, the flesh is still there, crying out for satisfaction. Trying to live like a nun in this day and age requires incredible amounts of will. This is a cosmopolitan university, and thousands of the men here subscribe to free love as their only religion.

What shall I do? I'm Christian but also human; my needs are the same as those of a man who prowls for a prostitute or those of a woman who sleeps with every guy in town. Before I ended my counseling relationship with Sarah last month, I asked her about this. She replied, "Do whatever you need to do to get your needs met without causing yourself guilt." Ha! A fine double-edged answer! Tell a Christian to go have an affair and not to feel guilty! Mark, you are right when you say that we are made for guilt. It does regulate our conscience. But it is also destructive, and how can we tell where one kind of guilt stops and another begins?

Sarah thinks I should have an affair because I doubt my desirability. She is right. We come back to the old bugaboo of acceptance. Still, I don't know if sex would affirm me or make me feel more awful. I'm dying to find out. I really am. The Bible's teachings on sexual behavior are so impossible; no one takes them seriously anymore, so why should I?

Do I really need sex? I think so. I ache to be filled, to have somebody complete me, to hold me and hold me and hold me until time runs out and there is nothing in the world but arms. I want to be touched, and how can I get touched at my age unless I get it sexually? Very few men will cuddle without expecting more, and I don't expect them to. They've been conditioned to think about their manhood in certain ways. Touching without intercourse is not one of those ways. Oh, to be touched. The one thing God can't do for me. If only my mom and dad had touched me . . . but we've been through all that before, and there's no point in repeating it.

From the depths of this pit of sexual desire, how do I dare raise my voice to God and ask for his help? It's hard to believe he really cares about it. Sure, God invented the body and thus the sex drive, but the church speaks for him, and the church says "cold baths and waiting, prayer and fasting." Are those realistic answers? Does it take a genius to see them for the evasions they are? I can tell you all about the reality. The reality is reading, working, teaching, then coming home drained to an apartment that echoes with emptiness and the feeling that life has passed by. Reality is a mirror that doesn't lie about my body, that tells me I am fat and undesirable and will never be wanted, so had better grasp whatever is available. I try to divert myself, to fill my mind with other things. I pick up magazines, even venerable news journals like *Time*, and see half-naked women enticing men to buy cars or cigarettes. I watch TV—more of the same. I go to movies and see people in bed more than out of it. I stroll across campus, with lovers on every bench and the bushes thumping. I try to concentrate on my work—and hear my office mates gossiping about last night's escapade and who is doing what with whom. I face students every day, mostly male, mostly older than me, mostly lonely, mostly all-too-ready to charm Teacher no matter what she looks like. I live this reality and ask myself how it can be borne. If I were Christ, I might find the control, but I am not a god. I'm not even a good little disciple like Paul. I'm a lonely woman in a sexy world, and I yearn to be accepted by that world. I'm getting old, and I want to be initiated, to learn what it is that they are all talking about and say is so wonderful.

After all, it's only a *little* sin. The church harangues us about fornication, but keeps silent about greed and pride and cynicism, which must be equally if not more abhorrent to God.

That was a fine piece of rationalization. You don't need to say so—I know when I am lying to myself. No sin can be taken lightly.

What it all comes down to is the easy talk about living out our faith clashing so profoundly with the agonizing attempt to *do* what we speak. If we really mean what we say about following Jesus, the way will never be easy for us, and every day is a new battle.

Love,
Hope

August 7, 1978

Dear Hope,

Jan and I just got back from taking the boys on a car trip through Nova Scotia. It was a welcome break. We did get your postcard from the Philippines before we left—it couldn't have happened to a nicer person. Considering your many talents and your concern for people, I wouldn't be surprised if such experiences become more and more frequent in your life. You don't have to *deserve* such experiences; they come your way because they help you to express the gifts you are developing. I'm delighted for you! I'll bet the experience will change your life in many more ways than you can see right now.

You spent a lot of time in your last letter asking some very difficult questions. This is usually my role— consider yourself a thief! You asked me about keeping a balance between the example of Christ and the socio-cultural conditioning which pulls in the opposite direction. I suppose I'd be famous if I could come up with a simple solution. As I reflect on this question, I believe the answer begins in my making a resolution in my own heart about my relationship with God and what it means. The standards which exist around me in the world are phony. I see this more clearly the older I get. The standards of the world are temporary; biblical standards are timeless. Now, that conclusion is not very concrete. For example, the choices I made ten years ago are not the ones I would make now, though I thought the past choices expressed God's desire for me and were made according to his Word. Knowledge of biblical standards deepens and matures as the Holy Spirit lets me grow in Christ.

Now what does all that have to do with sex? It's a perplexing issue, Hope. I work with a number of young women in their late twenties and early thirties who have not been married. Not that they would not make excellent wives—they would. But the plan of God for their lives has not led them to matrimony. Only recently a woman who had worked in the hospital for over twenty years finally found a man she wanted to marry. Why did it take so long? I just don't know. Yet she found a marvelous man to be her spouse in the many years remaining in her life. Is that unfair? All I can say is that we Christians can't let our lives be ruled by the standards of others, nor be slaves to the world's time-clock, which says we ought to be married at twenty-two. Rather, we must look to God's will for our lives and be responsible on that level. Not much comfort, is it?

Like you, I find that many churches exalt marriage. This biased approach is tragic because it completely misses the point of close interpersonal relationships. In a way the church is simply not dealing with the problems of human relationships at all. Instead it tries to solve the problems through socially acceptable channels. Don't be fooled about all those engineered marriages working. They do not, even those among faithful and devoted church members. Some of the things I hear from my married patients would curdle your blood. The church has failed these people by avoiding confrontation with the struggles of deep human contact. As a result, an awful lot of sexual problems among Christians remain well buried and ineffectively handled. Other Christians are struggling with the very problems you are facing right now, and God *does* care. Remember, if Jesus is who he says he is, a human in every way, then he too faced sexual temptation.

Do you really need sex? Isn't your comment about being wrapped in someone's arms the key to your true feelings? You have mentioned that there is a man in your life. Is your desire for him clouding your vision at this point and exaggerating the urges out of proportion? Would it help to go to some female in your church and tell her you need to be hugged and affirmed in touch? I know how difficult this would be for you, but I think it is preferable to plunging into the complications of a sexual relationship with a man. I'm unconvinced by your wistful comment that "it's only a little sin." If you believed that, you would have lost your virginity a long time ago.

As you walk past the thumping bushes and face the emptiness of your apartment, you are more in the hands of a comforter and guide than you realize. It takes time to build a relationship with God, to understand the reasons for his commands and to learn to delight in his love. But there he is, loving you through the struggle it takes to get to him. I ask you to consider something. Much of our correspondence is based on the same issue: despite your absolute intellectual conviction of God's love for you, you still have trouble feeling close to him and loving and trusting him. Any relationship you establish with a man— a human, fallible man—will be subject to the same inadequacies a hundredfold. How hard it would be for you to really accept and trust the love of a man!

In the world but not *of* it. We come back to this basic description of Christian life. It means that we do not buy into the cultural standards which try to define our lives for us. We have to be more responsible or, if you will, more free than that. We are climbing a different mountain with a different set of directions. This pertains not only to love and sex but to your concerns about Christian service as well. Should you race off to the wilderness and start digging irrigation ditches? Being a living witness in the midst of affluence is just as hard, if not harder. Sometimes, it is so easy to go to the people who have little and ignore those who have plenty, but the people with plenty have problems that are more complex and harder to combat.

If God wants you to be a missionary and live on fifty dollars a year, he will make that calling plain to you. You won't obey it out of a sense of obligation or guilt, but out of love and desire to do what is asked. Until you have this clear calling and the love to respond to it, be the best testimony you can be where you are. Loving God means going wherever he would have us go—the jungle, the neighborhood or Madison Avenue. Or, for that matter, celibacy. We must cling to him and stop identifying with possessions, with cultural standards or whatever else stands as an obstacle to his great and liberating light. Do you really feel that your lovely apartment and your stereo are worth dying for? Would you be devastated if they burned up in a fire? No? Well, that's the beginning of the godly attitude. Let go, let go, let go. Let go of everything the world tells you to cling to. You will never know the joy of God until you can give up everything for him, but you will be repaid abundantly for everything you sacrifice.

Depend on him. He will never cheat you. Remember that his grace is sufficient for everything.

I pray that this doesn't sound like more cheap talk to you. I do care for the difficulties you are facing and am hoping a response to this will come when you are able to write.

Love,
Mark

August 15, 1978

Dear Mark,

I need to talk with you about Daniel.

Though my mention of him has been fleeting, you have apparently sized up the situation. Your last letter has been forcing me to explore exactly what has been going on between him and me. Besides, since I last wrote, things have changed so much. My friend, I need your perspective.

Daniel. How do I describe him to you? A devil, a demon, the pus in a festering sore called a "relationship," an inconsiderate snob—and, at the same time, all of God that I may ever know. I love him with all my heart. I never knew how much until now.

We met last summer in the dining room of the graduate dorm where we both used to live. He had been living down the hall from me for ten months, but I can't remember ever noticing him until that night when a mutual friend invited him to sit at our table. At that first moment I felt a pained recognition, an instant explosion within me. Like something out of a Gothic novel, honest. Tall and fair-haired, blue-eyed and beautiful and articulate, he sat there and talked about philosophy while I felt my stomach twist and turn inside out. We talked for hours that night, and the talking has never stopped. I felt like I had met the other half, the missing part of myself. How can I find words for the mysterious bond that allows one to know the unvoiced needs of the other, the bond that allows one to interpret the catch in the voice and the posture that means "help me," the bond that grows out of shared interests and dreams and a sheer delight in being understood at last? It was almost as if a corner of my own mind were inhabiting another body and that I could not rest until I had claimed it. He, wonder of wonders, seemed to sense the same about me. I was in love, instantaneously in love. I was high, drugged on Daniel and addicted to him. Here, I thought, was the power to break down my walls. It was like drinking a sweet, delectable poison.

From that first minute there has been terrifying ambivalence. Daniel is brilliant, the most intelligent man I have ever met. A student of Nietzsche and Heidegger, he has utter contempt for God, but is fascinated by him too. He loves to toy with theological ideas, to tie me up in his sophistic webs, to mock and probe and challenge my faith. He senses that my adherence to absolutes gives me a strength that he lacks, and so makes me the dumping ground for all his insecurities and the shooting gallery for all his barbs. I have accepted this role rather uncritically because of my deep love for him... and also, I realize, because he appeals to my desire to play God. I have fancied myself the Messiah who could bring him to God, so that we could be married and live happily ever after. To that end, I have tried to "save" him by advancing him money to cover his financial irresponsibility, by bearing his burdens, by trying to be everything to him, by giving him unrestrained access to my time. Part of me has responded to this role of giving quite well, but the other part feels— you guessed it—cheated. Used. Rotten and worn-out. I want something from him. I want him to give as much as he gets.

Romance. I want romance from Daniel—the flowers and flirting and kissing. I want him to love me that way. But from the beginning he said, "It's not meant to be that way with us." Indeed, he admitted that he was sleeping regularly with another woman—"She doesn't mean much to me, but she's pretty and she wants it." He went on to admit that he had basically homosexual tendencies and was struggling over whether to indulge or not. I was ashamed by the intensity of my revulsion and disgust. But I accepted that because I love him. I wanted to stick by him no matter what, having as much of him as I could. And I thought it was all my fault. I wanted him so desperately, ached for him to fill me up, and instead he was sleeping with everyone but me—so it had to be my fat, my pimples, my awkwardness.

All during this past stormy year with Dan, I've continued my therapy and have encouraged him to go. Sarah and I spent a lot of time talking about Dan. Secular psychologists are so—you know, Mark—whatever feels good and all that. Being with Dan had really ignited me sexually for the first time. Never had I hungered for someone that way before, and I wanted to experiment with this new emotion. Sarah egged me on: "You have a right to get what you need . . . learn to love yourself and accept your body . . . get your needs met, it's okay." This, I knew, was not the way Jesus would have phrased it, but how tempting it was to be given permission. So I indulged myself a little. I guess I don't need to spell out how. Since Daniel resisted me and I didn't want anyone else, I "helped myself"—deliberate, willful sin, repeated again and again. Guilt overwhelmed me, but then I learned one of the sorriest lessons of growing up: sex is tricky and powerful, and once you start dabbling it's hard to assuage the hunger. So my desire increased, and my frustration with Daniel increased because he repeatedly refused to give me what I thought I absolutely had to have. Suddenly I found myself sexually aware of the whole world in a new way, and I had lost enough innocence to want the fulfillment of my fallenness.

Our needs for each other are such wildly differing needs. Thus he and I have gone through spells of intense intimacy punctuated by violent arguments that make us avoid each other until the pull becomes too strong. It's always fireworks between us, fire and ice, scarlet and purple—exhausting, thrilling and sick. It's always at fever pitch. There is nothing I don't know about Daniel. The deepest darkest secrets of his soul reside in me, and mine in him. Yet we never touch. Knowing that another woman possessed him in a way I never could, I have gone on ministering to him, supporting him, torturing myself with hopes I had no right to conceive. This, I wondered, is *agape?* Then Jesus was nuts to put himself through it, because it's hell!

Why do I write all this now? Because of the recent changes. And because of your last letter, which pointed out some truths to me. Because I am afraid. Because I need to give this away to God and trust him to deal with it.

A few weeks ago I had a big row with someone at my office over a project that I had initiated. She had taken charge of the project and, in my opinion, was handling it irresponsibly. After we argued I came home just devastated, my head throbbing with pain. I wanted the oblivion of pills, for Daniel and I had quarreled weeks before and were avoiding each other. But my other friends were unavailable, I had no pills in the house, and the pull to him was so strong. I knew he would understand. So I reached for the phone. When he said "Hello," I said, "Daniel," and he said, "Come right away." It really is that way with us, Mark.

I went and told him all about the argument. With his usual incisiveness, he analyzed the situation and helped me to see how I had let this one project get all tied up with my self-esteem. I was afraid to let anyone else try it another way because her way might be better, and then people would reject me. The old demon, rejection. Then I was really depressed about my vulnerability to this nemesis. Dan sat quietly watching me, neither of us speaking. Finally he looked at me penetratingly and said simply, "It's all right, Hope."

"It's not," I replied. "I feel like such an idiot."

"Cry." He took my hand in both of his. "You really need to cry." The tears began to fall instantly, not only from my emotional state, but from the feel of him. I wept and wept and wept. Dan pulled my face into his hands. Touching me. At last. I was being touched by this man who had come to dominate my world... this blond, beautiful man was touching *me*... there was such peace in it.

"I love you," he said.

My head came up. "What?"

"I love you."

A wave of fear and horror shot through me and

catapulted me out of my chair. He gripped me. Then I heard myself screaming, really screaming, "No, no, no! Stop it! You're killing me! Let me go!" I wrenched away from him and fled.

Dan followed, looking at me intently but without surprise. He reached to me. "Take my hand."

"I can't," I whimpered.

"You can. You *must*."

"No!"

He persisted. "Why can't you let me touch you? I want to."

"You liar!"

"Why don't you believe me?"

"I don't deserve it!"

Another old demon, the oldest of them all! I was appalled to hear myself say the words. Deeper than my education, my psychotherapy, my faith in the promises of Christ, is this thing that holds me back. How I ached to die then, to be free of it. I had begged for Dan's love, all the while believing that he would never give it to me because I was unworthy of him. Now he had challenged my old idea. He had shattered me, split me wide open, and I had run from him. He loved me... and now he would get his hands on the last part of me that was my own, tramp all over it and destroy me completely. I had no faith in his love. I didn't want to be cheated again... hurt again.

Dan got on his knees. "God," he said with some difficulty, "wants us to love each other." Then he began to pour forth. In the weeks since we had quarreled, he'd gone to a counselor, was wrestling through his sexual problems, had begun to pray. I could scarcely believe my ears. Then he reached his arms out to me and said, "Come to me. I want to hold you. Come."

Slowly I crept to him, and he folded me in his embrace. Clasped there, I had one of the most difficult conversations of my life. Together, we began to see how crippled we both are in our ability to love. Some horrible stuff came out. He pointed out to me how often I have insisted on walking alone at night on a campus noted for its high rape rate. "You hate yourself so much," he charged, "that you want to be beaten and mutilated, so you'll have proof of how loathsome you are." True, I acknowledged, I do have a fantasy of violent rape. And he has one of homosexual persecution. "You want to be whipped and abused," I charged, "because you think you're so abnormal that no one will accept you as you are." What a disaster sex would have been for us! To cope with sex, he had to distance himself so far that the woman could mean nothing. Thus he had never been able to make love to me, because I did mean something.

Where shall the healing come from to bind up these wounds? We both know that we can't love until we come to terms with the ultimate love of God, and we are praying for healing. Neither of us has yet dared to fully experience the words of Jesus, who says "Let me in. I love you. I know all about the sins and the fantasies and the sickness, and it's all paid for. I will never leave you no matter what happens. My love will transform you if you only let me in." Without faith in that, there can be no love.

Mark, I'm scared. I marvel at the changes in Dan and at the new tenderness in his treatment of me. I know that people cannot change overnight and that I am so impatient that I may interfere with this growth. I want us to be together so much that I have lost all my perspective. First John tells us that "perfect love casts out fear." The level of my present fear then indicates how far I have to go in learning the ways of love. Daniel and I have fought a violent battle this past year. We are both scarred from it. Now there is respite, but I do not know if it is peace or truce. I pray it is peace.

Please remember us in your prayers tonight and always.

Love,
Hope

August 30, 1978

Dear Hope,

This may sound silly, but the *concreteness* of your letter delights me, and I thank you for it. As hard as it may be for you to write about the feelings you are now having, the specificity is a tremendous help to me in understanding the process of growth that you are undergoing. I am moved that you trust me enough to confide these things.

I'm amazed at the way the relationship between you and Daniel has developed. Since you have been a little vague about him up to now, I had only the sketchiest sense of the intensity of it. I can see how Christianity's demand for honesty has had a profound effect on your bond with each other.

Your letter, in fact, enthralled me. I think it needs to be shared. Others are struggling with exactly the same problems, and they are just as fearful as you are. Perhaps your ability to articulate the situation could be a tremendous aid to them. So many young people are unable to let God work in their sexual problems. Your words give them a frame of reference for thinking about their own situations.

As far as guidance or assurance goes, there is little I can offer. Intellectually (as always) you know what you face. The battle will be to let the feeling side of you have confidence and trust. Know, *know* that God loves you both, and he will not bring his work to ruin. But his work may not always coincide with your desires. Think

97

of the course of your life now as a globe with paint dropping upon it. When or where or how fast the paint moves is out of your control, but it will eventually cover you completely and beautify you.

I can appreciate full well the horror you must have felt when Daniel spoke his words of love. As you grow, however, you are going to find that having someone give you affection will become increasingly comfortable and pleasurable. You'll discover that you don't have to *do* anything in response but accept it, and by that acceptance you'll let the other person know your happiness and reciprocation. This is indeed risky business, because the things that we do are our last defenses against really letting go to another person. When we stop trying to deal with reasons and actions and explanations and motives, we come to the terrain of unconditionality. We come to the core of ourselves and what we are.

Have I ever mentioned to you that I think Jesus hugged each one of his disciples at the Last Supper? How natural to want the arms of someone around you. It is one of the deepest and most ignored of human needs.

Janice and I will most certainly pray for you both in this time of uncertainty. Thank you for being so honest in your sharing. It really does encourage me in the work that I do and the relationships that I form.

And peace be with you, my dearly beloved sister.

Mark

September 6, 1978

Dear Mark,

I gave up all hope of sleep hours ago, and now at 5:00 A.M. I sit on the sofa listening to the rumbling of trucks on the highway, the chirping of the crickets, the gurgling of water in the pipes. How can life go on so routinely when I am poised on the brink of oblivion? Why does the world mock me with its everyday business, as though my trials matter so little? I sit here, because if I sleep I will dream and the dreams will torture me.

I want to know why love is so different from all that I was told about it. I want to know why love has to wound me so. And why the clock ticks on, reminding me that there can be no turning back for him or me or her. *Her!* He is with *her* tonight. He comes to me and says he loves me but he loves her too "in a way." He tells me that they are sleeping together again, that he doesn't want me that way "because it isn't right" with me. No, it's not right with me—but why is it right for him? When I sleep, I dream of her, breathless with rapture in his arms, and of him, being satisfied and sated by her. How, how can he love me and still do that, compartmentalize his needs and dole them out to specialists? How can he come to me for all but one of his needs, and then go to someone else for that all-important one and have the audacity to announce it to me as though I should commend him for his candor?

I feel like I ought to write a poem, but there aren't enough letters in the alphabet to tell about this grief or to make it rhyme. No language has enough meaning to express my despair. All the tear-filled eyes of the centuries cannot weep enough for my sorrow; there are not enough vacuums to hold my emptiness or enough dreamless sleeps to make me forget. I am so afraid. I fear that I will never have what she has with him, that I will not feel what they feel until I'm old and the burden of all the empty years has turned me bitter and cold. Your letter speaks exactly to the point, Mark. Daniel says it's nothing I have done; it's just the way things *are*. If I had done something, I could try to make amends or atone. But once again I am caught with the inescapable knowledge of my *is*ness, the thing I cannot change. He asked me to give that part of myself to him and I did, and this is my return. Love is horrible; it's a cheat, a liar!

I can only reach to my Lord, reach to the one who agonized in Gethsemane over the awfulness of love. Yet he knew he had the power to bring healing and fulfillment to those he loved so much. I am faced, on the other hand, by my terrible human finitude. Dan can nail me to a thousand crosses and I cannot redeem him. I can carry my burden all the way up to Calvary; I will collapse beneath it there and there will be no resurrection. Why, if God has begun to draw near to Daniel, can Dan so blithely resume his old ways? How can my love have so little effect? Why has God planted this love in me if I am only to suffer for it? I love Daniel! I will wither and die without him. God knows it—why is he tormenting me so?

I am so empty. My bed is empty, my arms are empty, my heart is empty yet brimming over with a love I want to give away, but which remains unclaimed. Is this what Jesus feels like with unrepentant sinners? Then truly he is a wondrous God to be able to bear so much rejection without bitterness. This one test has shown me how much I am unlike him.

Hope

September 11, 1978

My dear Hope,

I'm caught between appointments with only a couple of minutes to spare. I wish I had more time to respond to you. All I can say now is that the love you are suffering with is not unlike the terrible pain that afflicted your eyes. Neither seems logical, both resist definition and comprehension, both penetrate to the deepest part of you, so irreparably a part of your *is*ness that you simply have to live through them and wait on the Lord's answers.

Most of the things we've been taught about love —the poetry and flowers and moonlight—are just clichés. We've not been prepared to deal with issues like pain, trust, patience, but these are the stuff of love. That is why we must rely on God to help us through it, to make sense of it. I don't know why Daniel does what he does, and I wish that it didn't have to be this way for you. But I know that God is with you. He will sustain you—and even show you the positive aspects of this.

Know that you are loved, and be at peace.

Love,
Mark

September 24, 1978

Dear Mark,

It is finished. I have marched that horrible path to Calvary, and now there is nothing else but to say with my Savior, *"Finitus est. Pater in manus tuas commendo spiritum meum."* You are right, my friend. All the clichés are lies, and the happy ending is a myth.

When summer term ended, I had a couple of free weeks. I had to get away from here and sort some things out. First I went to Chicago to see an old friend, and then I wandered around in northern Michigan, thinking about the love that would not die despite all the betrayals it had endured, the love I could not kill. Staring into the placid blue water of Lake Charlevoix, I thought about the coming academic year, the new challenge of doctoral study, how being reconciled to Daniel was essential before any other steps could be taken, and how I quite simply loved him beyond all reason or sense. I tried to listen for God's voice, but he remained silent. I came back still restless and unrefreshed, but determined to see Daniel and to try to make things right.

As soon as I had let myself into the apartment and set down my bags, I reached for the phone. He seemed happy to hear my voice. "Would you like to come over and have dinner with me tomorrow evening?" he asked.

When he opened the door the next night, he gave me a genuine smile of warmth. "I wanted to see you last night, and I would have come to you," he said, "but... Sharon was here and I didn't know how to get rid of her."

103

I winced at that. "How is Sharon?"

"It doesn't matter. I've really missed you these last two weeks. It's made me see how much I like having you around. And how much I depend on you too."

Well, Mark, I could have died at that moment and counted my life complete. Daniel beamed at me and went off to set the table. We ate, then did the dishes together. Dan brewed an aromatic tea and set out an expensive liqueur in tiny crystal glasses. From the stereo came the soft strains of Bach's *St. Matthew Passion*, a piece that enthralls us both. A week earlier Dan had smelled a perfume that he thought would suit me—heliotrope, I think. He bought a bottle, which he now brought out, dabbling some on my neck and behind my ears. The touch made me tremble all over, and I said, "Dan, please don't tease me."

"Come here," he commanded. Together we curled up on the couch, and he wrapped his arms around me. For three hours we clung to each other, saying little, exclaiming over the music and getting high on the alcohol and on each other. In the midst of this I was so at peace and feeling such pleasure. I'd never had such a total sensual experience before—the nearness of a man, the feel of his skin, the sultry perfume splashed all over me, the trickle of exotic flavors over my tongue, the tenderness of Bach enveloping me.

I even prayed then. "God," I thought, "you have heard all my prayers. Thank you for this answer."

How quickly I had forgotten that two people share such communion at a great price. Dan and I were a long way from trusting each other, from trusting God, and we knew each other's weaknesses as well as strengths. I wanted to forget all the complications. I wanted even to forget that God's will might not coincide with mine. I wanted to think only of this moment, right now. So I pushed my luck.

"Daniel," I begged, "kiss me. Please. I want you so."

Dan stirred. "I was thinking of doing it. I really was. But I just can't. I have a feeling that I shouldn't."

"Why? I want you to do it."

"I know. But... it doesn't seem right with you."

There we were again. *With me.* Anger flared through me and I snapped, "Why? You were with her last night—have you forgotten how already?"

He reared back, then pushed me away. "You never stop harping on me! You know damned well what the limits are. I've spelled them out to you a dozen times, and you just keep pushing, pushing, pushing for more."

"Me? You bastard! It's always what *you* want, things have to be the way *you* say, and you won't give a thing to anybody else! Always looking out for Number One! After everything I have done for you..."

"You had both eyes open," he spat back. "I never promised you anything. You knew about Sharon a long time ago, and that's the way you're going to have to take me, because..."

I ache to remember it. All the doubt came pouring out, the old pain was dredged up, and we took pleasure inflicting it on each other. We alternated the roles of tormentor and victim—I turn pale with shame now at the words that crossed my tongue. I wanted to abuse him, to watch him writhe. His eyes glinted with malice and disgust.

"Sharon, Sharon, Sharon!" I screamed. "How many others are there? Are there little boys too?"

"You're jealous," he taunted. "Jealous of me. Because I can have her and anybody else I want. And who would want you, the way you look?!"

I gasped, then flung out my hand and slapped him across the face with all the power I could muster. The violent crack echoed throughout the room. Then suddenly, all the fire went out of me. I sat down, and felt *something* beside me. Dan's eyes widened, telling me that he sensed it too. He sat at my feet. As I reflect back now, I can think only of the verse that says, "Be still, and know that I am God." We were still for a few minutes. Then he was opened to me. I felt that I could read all that was in his mind and that he could read mine. We looked at each other, and I felt all the pain and struggle within him as he could feel mine. Tears came from our eyes. "We're killing ourselves," I sobbed at last. "We are determined to destroy each other."

Dan choked. "It's horrible. We have to get help, we have to let God in . . ."

"We have to be apart for a while," I said, gaining new insight from the Thing that hovered near me. "This is not the time for us."

He nodded. "Yes. You are right. Hold me for a minute, then go."

I embraced him, and out the door I walked, stumbling home but not understanding what Force propelled me. Almost immediately the assurance of that Presence banished from me. So now I am alone, unable to call or see or even write him because of the covenant we made to be apart.

You know what I feel like? I feel crucified. My life's blood has seeped away. Unlike Christ, I have no awareness of coming Easter. I've descended into the hell of unlovedness. Dante was right—it's cold, with the howling winds of alienation covering it with snows of death. I don't know whether I should hope for a reunion with Dan, or whether it was hopeless from the beginning, or if he misses me as much as I ache for him. I'm doomed not to know. And I hurt so.

You cannot comfort me, Mark. I don't expect you to, and I don't want to get a reply from you just yet because any words would sound petty and trivial to me. There is nothing anyone can do for me right now—except maybe to pray and ask God what he is trying to teach me through what feels like the greatest tragedy of my life.

Hope

IV
HIS GREAT BIDDING

Therefore to his great bidding I submit.

Milton/Paradise Lost 11. 314

November 27, 1978

Hi, Mark,

I've been silent longer than usual this autumn, haven't I? Has it been a busy one for you too? I've discovered that doctoral programs are significantly different from lowly M.A. tracks, and I feel like I have to be even more serious than before. So plenty of midnight oil has burned these last two months. There's been the hassle of assembling a guidance committee, getting a research topic defined and preparing for the specter of comprehensive exams sometime in the future. My biggest stumbling block is going to be the two language competency exams I have to pass. Though I've studied both French and Latin, I've let them slide and now have to learn them all over. Part of me rebels at this. I know that fluency is needed for my research, but learning Arabic or Russian or Chinese would be so much more practical.

I bury myself in all this scholarly activity not only to get the work done but to keep from thinking about Daniel, and sometimes I almost succeed. God seems to have decreed total silence and separation as the way of healing. I wish it didn't have to be so radical—but then, I seldom get my way with God. Will this discipline really polish the carbon of my surface into a sparkling diamond of righteousness? It's so hard to rejoice in obedience sometimes. I earnestly pray that I will be better for all this. Meanwhile, on weekends you can find me playing Vivaldi masses and fervently raising my own voice in the *dona nobis pacem.*

I don't mean to sound crude, Marcus, but have you ever found yourself wanting to pray "God damn you, God"? I have always believed that it's good to plan your life and know where you're going, but since God entered my life he's done nothing but throw curve balls and make messes of my neat plans. It's so easy to get discouraged. For years I have wanted to be in a library, unearthing the theoretical foundations of English satire—now I'm there and it's not enough; I yearn for more. I wanted my own apartment and academic success; I have these, but everybody else's grass looks greener. And God could make everything right. With a stroke of his mighty hand he could deliver me from all my demons and show me what to do with my life. He could give me Daniel back. He could make my Latin as good as Cicero's. And he could make me stop wanting to have sex. But he sits in heaven inscrutable, and lets me enjoy the benefits of being a free person with a free will. What a paradox it is!

So I have to say, thank God for his Body. I've had my battles with the church in the past, but some true guidance and help does come from the members who assemble in his name. I've been depending on my church more than ever this term, since the affair with Dan has left me subject to so many emotions. I feel worthless and unloved and unlovable, ready to leap at whatever will pay some attention to me. The unforced and unpretentious acceptance I feel with some people in my church has kept me going. Also, some plain-talking folks have kept me from making some really stupid mistakes.

For example, this term I have a rare specimen in one of the advanced composition classes I'm teaching. He

is a charming Iranian sociologist here to do advanced degree work, and he sits in front of my eyes every day. Honestly, I've never met a student more intelligent or moti-
vated or hard-working—or a man with so much sheer vis-
ceral attraction. He literally makes my mouth water.

Masoud is a few years older than me and makes
no secret of the fact that he thinks I am wonderful. Partly
he is homesick and thus responding to the nurturing style
I have in the classroom; partly he is impressed that I know
what's going on in that part of the world and can talk in-
telligently about it. But there is also some plain old male/
female stuff at work. He has made it obvious that I can
call the shots with him, and it's been so tempting. I think
to myself: "Why not? He's adorable and he wants me, so
why shouldn't I help myself? Who will I hurt?" Oh, Mark,
when I am left to myself, I can do such a great job of con-
ning myself!

What an amazing capacity for delusion we
humans have! At such times, only the Spirit through his
church can save us from our own folly. With sin on my
mind, I crawl into my Friday-night Bible study and settle
down for a chat with my friend Mary, who's divorced and
pretty knowledgeable about the ways of the world.
"Mary," I say, "the tension is getting too high. I have to
decide what to do with Masoud."

"Indeed," Mary replies. "Your chief concern
must be whether you will dishonor God in anything that
you choose to do."

I squirm a bit. I don't want to admit that I have
been manipulating the man through my position as his
teacher. "Oh . . . I think it's a very positive thing for Chris-

tians and Muslims to have meaningful dialog..."

Mary hoots. "Dialog! Don't give me this stuff about all your ecumenical principles; I wasn't born yesterday. You want to sin for a season, that's all."

"Mary," I protest, "I have needs. Daniel left me high and dry, and I just have to take care of myself."

"Are you willing to sacrifice a steady diet of protein for a quick high on sugar?"

"What's protein? This hell God is putting me through?"

"He knows what he's doing. You know that. You know righteousness means more to you than this lust you feel at the moment."

"But Masoud is gorgeous and smart, and he wants me..."

"God wants you too and has a better claim."

Of course she is right. It's good to be reminded even when it's hard to listen. Even more, I know Mary can be trusted because she is in Christ, part of the church that ministers to me.

Mark, I wish the best holiday to you and Jan. You've been such a blessing to me, and this season reminds me of that. In these days of Advent, let us join hands and celebrate as the children of God.

Love,
Hope

December 4, 1978

Dear Hope,

I just got your letter. I've been under a huge pile of work too. Though I've been working desperately to extricate myself, the light at the top is still awfully dim. Gradually I've been trying to pull back from some responsibilities to give myself time to think, write and regroup. I guess I'm the classic case of an overextended person. I'm no longer counseling students at Harrisville, and I also stopped teaching part-time at Grant College so that I could devote more time to the hospital. I enjoy doing so many things that I get annoyed by my human limits. God has blessed the various areas of my work so much that it's hard to give them up, but I am so fragmented from trying to keep up with everything that I am losing control of it all. So it's time to withdraw and be refreshed.

I'm intrigued that my gradual withdrawal has brought to the forefront the talents and gifts of others who can take over for me. Then I have to acknowledge to myself that it would be an act of pure selfishness to try to hold on to everything because I feel like it's my "kingdom." Others can do equally well what I have done; I must let them have a chance at it.

Even though you asked me not to write, Hope, you haven't been far from my thoughts. Time and again you have come into my mind, and I have wanted to write to you so badly. But other priorities swept in and forced me to push aside things I wanted to do. Keep writing to me. It brings great joy to my day to see a letter with your return address in my box. Even though the letters are sometimes full of sorrow, as September's was, I love to read them.

I thank God that you have friends there who can head you off at the pass. Hug Mary for me, and tell her I thank her for watching over you. We all need friends who will level with us. They are the ones who tell us the truth about ourselves that we would rather not hear.

I'm at a loss to say anything about you and Dan and these tremendous desires you have for a sexual relationship, though I have seen the same thing often enough in my patients. How I wish that Christians could shed their hang-ups and hug one another in the context of fellowship! The tactile contact would, I believe, go a long way in affirming everyone's physical identity. Some congregations do this, but even there it can have sexual overtones. And there's not much we can do about that in a fallen world, is there?

You ask me whether I ever pray in great anger toward God. Oh, yes. Yes, yes. Sometimes I find myself walking with head down in corridors that seem to have no end. Because my head is down, though, I don't see the doors along the corridor where someone is standing and saying to me, "Why not walk this way for a while and keep me company?" I am so intent on reaching the end of the corridor (as I perceive it) that I don't realize I have been offered a new direction for my energy and resources.

Shall I be specific? As I said, I have been struggling tremendously with paperwork and patient contacts which seem to go on and on. My administrative responsibilities are mushrooming. I keep thinking I have to re-structure my job a little, but there is never time. So I feel burned-out and fretful with God. Suddenly, out of the blue has come a letter inviting me to come to South Africa for a month to deliver some lectures. Never in my wildest dreams did I think of something like that happening to me! How much like your trip to Asia last summer! So here I am, thinking of passports and visas for Janice and me so that we will be ready to go sometime in the next year. I don't know why this has happened, but it's clearly one of God's opportunities. We Christians are not in the busi-ness of figuring out our lives by ourselves or for ourselves. We must always be ready for the call.

Christianity teaches that the faithful steps of the righteous will avail much, but those steps can seem awfully plodding. As you walk your corridor, Hope, lift up your head to look for the doors on the side. Try to re-member that you are living in the presence of God and thus cannot be forgotten. I've just been going through this feeling because so many members of my staff have left just as I was getting to know and like them. Perhaps I will never see them again. I feel so much pain when they go and worry about finding new ones to replace them. I want to close myself off from learning to know others so I won't have to endure the agony of more separation in the future. So I must remind myself that God is always with me and will never leave me.

That, incidentally, is another reason your letters mean so much to me; I know that our relationship con-tinues. Even though I see you hurting, your level of un-derstanding about spiritual things and a value system higher than earth's stirs me deeply. Thank you for struggling. It encourages me. Write me again soon, and try not to get caught in the red tape that tends to be cut lengthwise rather than across in academic circles!

Love,
Mark

January 3, 1979

Dear Mark,

Happy New Year to you, my sage and wonderful friend! What nice words you say! Let me assure you that the comment about my letters bringing joy to your day is exceedingly mutual. When I get to the mailbox and see one of those heavy, cream-colored envelopes from Sanctuary, my heart leaps up!

Soon I will be two years old in Christ. I suppose that means I am entering my terrible twos. God has been faithful through all the slobbering and babbling of my infancy. It comforts me to call him Mother in my prayers sometimes. Do you think that's irreverent? God to me is a warm, loving thing that cuddles me a lot and leans over me while I am sleeping.

Though but a spiritual baby, I am no child. I'll be twenty-five by the world's time clock this summer—a fourth of a century. Thinking about this approaching milestone has raised several points that I would like to discuss with you. All of them seem to be pulling me toward one conclusion—it is time to leave the academic world.

When I think about getting a Ph.D., what comes into my mind? The gown. The chevrons. The velvet and bright colors of the hood. The slow pompous marches while the organ echoes with the stately measures of a baroque tune. To want those things strikes me as self-indulgent. In fact, being a grad student is one big exercise in self-indulgence. I love the trappings, the flexible hours, the stimulating university environment, the witty people, the challenge of working with ideas. But the longer I am here, the more I see the side of it that I don't like—and that is not good for me. Academe is overrun with people who stand for nothing, who are obsessed with themselves and with publishing silly articles that no one reads, who care only for prestige and very little about the practical applications or moral implications of literary analysis. I don't want to become like them. How ironic that the humanities, the conscience of civilization, attract such people! But in departments of literature, art, music, philosophy, history—there we find the stuffed shirts, the stinkers, the narcissists who mold their graduate students in their own images. No one cares about ethics or decency; no one will compromise or sacrifice anything that affects his position; no one speaks out about the illiteracy or hunger or spiritual emptiness that afflict our planet. And these are the issues that demand response in our time. I fear that I too am beginning to make this set of warped values my own. Who am I helping by cranking out papers on the structure of the Neoclassic couplet or the genesis of comic realism in Jane Austen's novels? I have a lot of contempt for my work these days.

Ostensibly, this work is equipping me to teach in college someday. But the chance of my getting a job teaching literature is virtually nonexistent in a time when Harvard and Yale grads are working as waiters. There are just too many of us in a world where fewer and fewer people are going to college. Then, too, I don't know if I *want* to teach literature for the rest of my life. I've had great fun teaching grammar to Arabs. Oh, I love my scholarly studies, love the reading and the integrating and the thinking, but I don't believe I will feel cheated if I never get to unveil the mysteries of Chaucer to undergrads. So how necessary is it to go on with this? I'm not dedicated to becoming a professor, and a Ph.D. in English will overqualify me for everything else.

Of course, not all my reasons for wanting to leave are so lofty and intellectual. The deadlines, the long hours in the library, the fretting over grade-point averages and the living at the whim of bureaucrats and state legislatures who can take away my funding with one stroke of a pen— this wearies me. Also, I worry about getting so locked in to academic life that I won't be able to leave. There are so many people here in town who have been hanging around for twenty years because they can't let go of college memories. I don't want to be like them! Does my attachment to the place and the advantages it offers rob me of some of my freedom to act for Christ? Am I exerting my will over his by clinging to a place because I'm scared to move?

Then, too, there is Daniel. I am tired of avoiding certain places, of wondering whether I will run into him when I get on a bus or walk in the research stacks. This town is not so large that two people can avoid each other indefinitely. Getting real physical distance between us may help bring healing to me. So many things here remind me of him. When I walk past a certain building or garden I remember walking there with him. My apartment is full of associations with him. I want to stop remembering; new faces and places may help.

But if I leave, where can I go? Only here can I do what I really do best: work with words and organize data and write. God gave me these gifts, but the university is the only place that values them. Or is it? Like you, am I walking in a corridor where I forget to look up for the windows and doors at the sides? Maybe I need to ask myself whether I have given God a chance to show me what else I can do for him. How can I go about asking this? I don't know where to turn. My skills are not the kind that list themselves neatly on a résumé. I can't program computers or fix drains. So many employable skills are beyond my ken.

The knowledge of different cultures that I have learned from my students, the ability to wrestle with intellectual problems, the capacity to provoke thought in others—I want to take these gifts outside the ivy halls and see what happens. Yet I am afraid. I've been in school all my life, and it is all I understand. Leaving here will also open me to charges that I was too dumb or too lazy to finish my degree. Such accusations would destroy my self-esteem. Leaving will remove me from the intelligentsia and force me to deal with new kinds of people. Leaving frightens me. But I must conquer that fear; in fact, it practically forces me to leave so that I can.

What is my calling? How can I know? If my calling is not to write a thesis on Augustan poetic diction, is it to join the foreign service or write speeches or wait on tables? I am at a loss. I know that some people manage to serve God valiantly within academe. Certainly Christians are needed here among the pagans and the scoffers. But I feel a raging fire within me to move on—I am filled with the ideas of dead men that I want to offer to the living. I want to test all my theories and notions and dreams in the arena of real life. The years are slipping away, so I dare not dawdle on forever.

Meanwhile, as you pray with me for guidance, I will do what the Lord has given me to do, here and now. I will teach as effectively as I can, do my dummy literary study with some integrity and pray for the spring thaw. In this frozen January I am anxious to see what roses will be blooming by my birthday.

Love,
Hope

February 2, 1979

Dear Hope,

Here's another cream-colored envelope for you!

It's interesting that you describe your relationship to God as one moving in the direction of nurture. Certainly God has a mothering side; otherwise, Christ would not have said, "Let the children come unto me, for such is the kingdom of heaven." Too often we emphasize the intellectual aspects of God over the nurturing ones. We have to remember that God is complete and that all his resources are available to us.

I will never outgrow my need for nurture. When I have reached out to people and have been slapped in the face, I have to be reassured of God's love for me. Then I don't get lost in trying to have other people meet my needs when they can't or don't want to. For this reason I dearly love the Psalms. The writers speak again and again about their loneliness and isolation. Then, as they reflect on God's actions in history and in their lives, the assurance of his care resurges in them and they find new energy to carry on.

With that as my preface, I now want to respond to the questions you have so carefully outlined in your letter. Janice and I have talked about this, and she echoes my own feelings about your concerns. I'm going to respond in an order which indicates a sifting process, so that you can stop anywhere along the way that seems most reasonable.

First, I operate on the assumption that you have

123

the intellectual, emotional and spiritual freedom to leave the academic scene anytime you want to. I would respect that choice if you made it. I don't want to impose specific directions for your personal development. Rather, I hope I can clarify alternatives to you so that you make the best selection. Whatever you decide is between you and God alone. Don't live your life to suit anyone's value system except your own.

Second, the desire to express yourself through writing and words is a most admirable thing to do. The gifts God has given you indeed need to be shared in a world where Christianity is so easily shoved aside and where Christians desperately need encouragement to deal more adequately with the struggles of the world. Your task, as I see it, is to find the way to use those gifts at the highest level without worrying how many people you touch. Those who *want* to be reached *will* be reached.

Third, I would raise this question about continuing your doctoral program. (I struggled with exactly the same question ten years ago.) Are you so mired down in your current slough of despond that you no longer have a clear vision of what's ahead? You see, the middle years of grad school are very tunnellike, and almost everybody goes through a period of wondering and reassessment. You are correct that academe is overrun with people who stand for nothing. But don't assume that you will become like them, especially since you have God's Spirit within you. It's so unfortunate that the academic world at the graduate level is almost totally divorced from Christian experience. Few church-related or Christian colleges offer graduate programs of any kind. This worries me, but I don't know what to do about it. When I was still teaching part-time at Grant, I saw how many students hungered for a Christian perspective on literature and psychology beyond the undergraduate level. And there are no Christian grad programs in English, and very few in psych, for them to go to. By completing your Ph.D. you may be able to step into an area where no one is standing either in the secular or the Christian academic structure.

Fourth, if you leave school and establish a career that uses your verbal talents, can you be as effective as you want to be? Would a break from school for a year or two accomplish the same thing as a complete break? During a leave of absence you would gain a much broader experience of the world without severing all your old ties. I took a break before I went to grad school, and what I gained during that time was invaluable to me. I guess I am cautioning you about finality at this point. Keep in mind that you still have to ascertain what audience you wish to reach. Perhaps you will need the carrying card of a Ph.D. in order to be heard by certain people, if you decide it is they you wish to minister to.

Fifth, praying for the spring thaw happens not only in school but wherever you are. What you feel now, you will feel again. So don't look to leaving school as a panacea for all your problems. Every corner of life has its ebb and flow and its time for hitting bottom . . . and coming up again.

Sixth, don't worry about making wrong decisions. All your decisions will either open more doors or lead to closed doors. You asked me how you can find your calling. I can only say that you are in the will of God anytime you make a choice. No longer do I believe in the idea of lives following fixed paths. I don't mean that we should follow immoral or unethical paths, but rather that we will be presented with multiple opportunities to use our gifts. So we have to make the best decisions we can at any given time and live with the results, knowing that God is always with us. Our task is also to make the best of whatever good, bad or indifferent results we get from our decision. No matter what decision I make, it will reflect my relationship with God even if I run into a dead end. The question then becomes: How do I handle the dead ends and what use can I make of them?

I don't know if any of this will be of much help to you, but I hope you ponder it. Jan and I will pray, as always, and look forward to another letter. Thank you for the intensity with which you share yourself.

With loving concern,
Mark

March 6, 1979

Dear Mark,

The resolve to leave has become firmer in the last couple of months. Your letter helped a lot. Thank you for taking so much time to help me. The part about taking a leave of absence was something that had not occurred to me before. My dissertation director was happy with that idea. He understands my current dissatisfaction and thinks that getting away would be good for me, but also declares that I am a "born scholar" and will want to come back. Part of the discontent, in his view, is that the program here is too easy for me. Perhaps he is right; I work hard, but I certainly could be challenged more.

Though I'm still wavering, I took a couple of pieces of concrete action related to leaving. Last week I had an interview with a woman who directs a program for volunteers-in-mission in Taiwan. It's church-related, involving a one-year commitment to teaching English and doing student outreach while living totally immersed in the culture. The volunteers live in dormitories with Chinese students in Chinese neighborhoods, and there are few Americans around those districts to socialize with. I approve of that. My experience with international students here has shown me that one never becomes acculturated if he stays with his own kind. As a trained teacher of English as a second language, I'd be very welcome in this program. The director told me they usually can't get trained personnel because we can make so much money working for other organizations. I don't know, Mark. It's a subsistence-level salary only, and Taiwan is so far away. But on the other hand, maybe my attraction to living abroad was inevitable. God didn't put me in this line of work by accident. Though I initially was horrified by the teaching, I've learned to love it; now I have expertise, and here comes an opportunity. And isn't it odd that less than a year ago I had my little trip to Asia, so that the experience of traveling trans-Pacific and being in hot weather won't be totally new to me? Hmmm. Curiouser and curiouser. Well, it's something to think about.

I did speak with the placement service here on campus about career advice, but their approach appalled me. After telling me I was an idiot for having pursued liberal arts all these years, they told me to sign up for some courses in computer programming or accounting, throw together a résumé that de-emphasized my philosophical background and start selling myself. That terminology speaks so much to what is wrong with this consumer society. Everything is a commodity, including people, and the person with the most worth is the one who holds a prestigious and lucrative position. I prefer to do my career planning without the aid of such narrow-minded experts. I have enough confidence in the Wonderful Counselor to know that computer programming is not a gift he has given me and that he does have a place for me even if I did major in the humanities.

As I grow in Christ, I understand more clearly what it means to belong to him, really belong. The metaphor of the vessel is so helpful and powerful to me. We are filled by the Spirit, emptied by life's trials, refilled again from the endless depths of God's love. But at all times we remain just the containers, wrought by the Artist of Artists. When I forget who I belong to, I find myself in a mess from which only grace can redeem me. I am cracked, broken, flawed by my sin; but then my Maker comes to remold me to my original beauty and fill me again. If only all people could accept the beauty of this concept. So often I want to hold the world in my arms and weep over it as I tell it what I know.

I say that in light of what was a moment of excruciating pain for me. Daniel was here the other night. He materialized on the doorstep one night after I had gone to bed. I struggled into my robe and opened the door, and when I saw who it was my heart dropped down to my toes. The icy, clear blue eyes caught mine. "Can I come in?" he asked as he strolled across the room and sat in his favorite chair.

Trembling idiotically, I said, "I'm glad to see you."

"How have you been, Hope?"

"So-so. Working hard. Daniel, why have you come here?"

Without ceremony, he asked bluntly, "Do you still love me?"

Within me, waves started to roll. Could he be coming back to me after all these months? Was God going to reward me at last for my faithful love of Daniel? "Oh!" I burst out. "You don't need to ask. It's written all over my face. I'd still follow you to hell!"

"I was afraid of that." His voice was hollow, but it wasn't a forced hollowness. He might have been talking to a dentist about a cavity. "Well, I don't love you.

I wonder if I ever really did. Anyway, there is nothing left. And I don't want you to sit here cherishing any hopes about me. We are beyond reconciliation. I want nothing to do with you, ever."

"Get out," I said.

For a while I sat nursing my shock. Then I wept the bitterest tears of my life, tears of confusion and agony. I cried out to God like Job, Jeremiah, Moses and Hosea combined. I prayed to die as I used to pray when my eyes hurt. I prayed that God would strike Daniel dead, but even more I prayed for my own death. Only when I die, I thought as I clenched fistfuls of sheet, will I be held in arms that will never abuse or betray me. So let me die. But I didn't die. I slept. I woke up and went to work, and the world looked the same as it had the day before.

A couple of nights later, the doorbell rang late one night. I fought off the stab of fear that went through me and answered it. There stood a woman who works in my office. "Can I come in?" she asked pathetically. I hesitated. She's been in unstable emotional shape ever since her marriage broke up three years ago and her husband got custody of their daughter. Throughout these years she has seen a psychiatrist weekly, been committed to an institution once and performed three carefully orchestrated suicide attempts. Gradually her friends have all turned away from her because she drowns them in her misery and makes incredible demands on their time and resources. I knew all this. But here she was, and she was weeping, so I let her in and put on the teapot.

She began to pour forth immediately. "My parents never hugged or touched me... you can't imagine how horrible that is... I needed love but didn't know where to get it, so I looked to my teachers... I became a model student to please them, because they gave me the affirmation I never got at home... but it was never enough ... my husband never understood my need and he ran away from me... I feel so empty, every minute emptier than the last... I'm so alone, no one loves me, I wish I were dead."

My heart turned over. Another version of my own anguish. Truly there is nothing new under the sun. "Why have you come to me tonight?" I asked her.

She looked at me from her tear-ravaged face and choked, *"You?* Why not you? You are so beautiful; you give so much to others. You flow over with generosity and compassion... like a fountain with a source that never runs dry. People flock to you—don't you know that? You seem to have an endless reserve of love to give. My students hate me, but yours adore you. I hear them talking. They say that you care about them. How do you show them that? God! God! I wish I were you!"

From the depths of my own emptiness, I felt God's limitless love fill me up. The new wine drenched me. Mark, do you remember saying a long time ago that I reminded you of a wellspring under pressure, and all I needed was to take the cap off? What an affirmation her words were! Daniel had drained me to the dregs, leaving me a vessel utterly dry, and here came the new supply flowing in and giving me life again. Resurrection. Life in Christ is a continual coming back from the dead. This God of ours does not give up. When I realized that this woman had come to me of all people for nurture, I saw that God had put me in his chain of command to love the world and that there could be no turning back for me. *Me* with all my inadequacies and fears and evils. I am commissioned to love.

In these bleak days of uncertain future, when the chill factor seems a symbol of life's bitterness, I remember that those who sow with tears shall reap with joy. As we are filled from above, we grow readier to serve. And thus we can face whatever decisions are ahead with a settled heart.

Love,
Hope

April 7, 1979

Dear Mark,

Easter approaches, the time of new beginning, the season of promise. It's a tender season in Michigan. The magnolias overcome their shyness and burst forth, the lilacs preen themselves triumphantly, the trees break out all over with that lacy green growth that surrounds the blue sky with a filigree frame. (I'm sitting in the horticultural garden at the moment; thus the poetry!) The lilies remind us that we have been justified and may be at peace.

My days here are numbered; that's why it all seems so precious. I'm going to do it, Mark. I've been accepted into the Taiwan teaching venture, and I'll be departing from San Francisco in late June for my orientation to the Orient. It's going to be the most frenetic, fascinating and frustrating year of my life. The decision was surprisingly easy when the offer came. I had applied for a few other jobs, but my heart wasn't in them, and this one had the exotic flavor that part of me hungers for. Saying yes was easy. I suspect that it is the only thing that will have been easy when I look at the experience in retrospect!

In Taiwan my master's degree will enable me to have a professorship in a college, and I'll also be expected to teach English and Bible studies at night. I feel some timidity about teaching Bible, but I'm ready to try. The information packet says I will have to learn to communicate in Mandarin, eat with chopsticks all the time, do all my laundry by hand (!), learn to coexist peacefully with lizards and mosquitoes—and maybe rats. I will have to get used to power outages and water shortages, to riding a bike everywhere (I don't think I've been on a bike since 1965), to constant filth in my surroundings. Have I ever been, at any time, selfless? No! This is going to be an entirely new type of education for me!

Everyone is appalled. My parents, of course, say little; they are used to my independence from them. But my sisters think I am insane. (My announcement phone call to them was interesting; one of my sisters thought Taiwan was in Africa.) My secular friends and colleagues are shaking their heads and telling me how much money I could make in Saudi Arabia. But the church here is enthusiastic and already organizing a support group for me. Heaven's logic tells me that whatever material deprivations I undergo will make me richer than before—if I can hack it. I must remember, now and forever, that in the Christian life there are no solo flights and no solitary daredevil leaps over canyons of crises. A firmer hand does the steering and lets us enjoy the scenery, as a voice reminds us that we can't enjoy the scenery until we *look* at it. If we keep our eyes tightly shut until we come down safely, we will have missed what we went up to see.

Even as I tremble at the unknown I am about to face, I feel a sense of rightness about taking the step. If my life has been lovingly engineered to prepare me for this, I am ready to go with gladness and gaiety. Leaving my network of friends will be painful indeed. I am reminded of what you wrote a few letters ago about the agony of separation. I will have to leave people I love, professors I respect and admire, the church that nursed me through my conversion, material things that I treasure. It all has to be pared down to two suitcases and a memory. I don't know a soul over there. It's one place in the world where Daddy can't come and get me if something goes wrong. There's not even an embassy there anymore. What happens if I get homesick or horribly ill, or if I accidentally break a law and get thrown into jail, or . . . what if, what if? I suppose the answer there is the same as it is here—his grace will suffice.

The church, as I said, is being incredibly supportive and praying with me for the success of this mission. Something happens when people pray, something unspeakably powerful that weaves us all together in an invisible fabric that only our souls can see. I feel right now like I am being fortified. This Holy Spirit we believe in, this mysterious force, is in me, and in you, and in Taiwan, which means that you are there even when you are here, and I'm here when I'm there. What a paradox! What a delight! What an unbreakable source of strength we have access to!

So many things need to be done. I have to get a visa, inoculations, someone to sublet this apartment, places to store my furniture and my books. I need to keep up with my teaching, to set aside time for my friends. When I first contemplated leaving the university, I pictured myself moving toward the security of a real job, a car, a bay window and a dog, not this quixotic rushing in where angels fear to tread (literally—Taiwan is covered with snakes!). It's all happening so fast now that I feel breathless. It will settle as I get used to it. Over the next two crazy months, I'll rely on your prayers as I prepare. So much of the prayer we have prayed has helped me to find this opportunity, just as the therapeutic work we did formed the links in the chain which now binds me to God. You are going as much as I am. Blessed Easter, my friend, and write to me soon.

Love,
Hope

May 28, 1979

Dear Hope,

I am sorry for not getting back to you sooner! The spring has been a frantically busy one, and Janice and I have been getting ready for the Africa gambit, which starts (coincidentally) in late June. I feel anxious over the workshops and lectures I'll be presenting, and I think that in some ways I am trying to prepare for situations that can't be prepared for. Of course I won't be staying a long time abroad as you will, but I need prayer too—that God will work in me through this experience and guide me.

The decision you have made will open more doors than you dream possible. The Holy Spirit will be a steady source of refuge and power in what lies ahead of you. Is your imagination running wild, manufacturing more of those terrifying *what ifs*? This is a defense mechanism we all have, to anticipate the worst possible conditions that could occur, so that what really does happen will be less of a trauma for us. Have no fear; the Spirit will guide you to good people there. An old friend of mine was a missionary in Taiwan for many years, and he had the highest praise for the Taiwanese people. You will find other citizens of the kingdom of God to replace those you are giving up.

Indeed, the idea of being God's citizen brings comfort to me and, I hope, to you too. Don't try to represent the United States in an atmosphere as charged with political unrest as Taiwan's. Remember that if you let your citizenship rest in heaven, you will always be secure.

You have so much to offer to this experience, and

I believe that you have also the patience and tenacity to go below the surface and to really make a difference in the lives of the students you will be teaching. You have the curiosity and the interest to become a truly bicultural person and the grace to accept what will be strange to you. Jan and I will pray for you regularly. Our affection for you has not lessened in the least, despite the dearth of letters in your box lately. Please keep us informed of your whereabouts and what happens to you. I long to maintain my ties with you throughout the next year and beyond.

With all the prayers I can muster at the moment, may the peace of our Father and the freedom of Christ and the comfort of the Spirit be with you now.

Love,
Mark

June 23, 1979

Dear Mark,

I'm in a jet high above the earth on my way to California. I was home with Mom and Dad for a few days after an incredible leave-taking from Michigan. What an outpouring of parties, presents, prayers and love. How blessed I have been! But I have no regrets. The land to which I now go is the home that has been prepared for me.

In Exodus 15 there's a passage of extraordinary beauty that Handel adapted in *Israel in Egypt:* "Thou shalt bring them in, and plant them in the mountain, in the sanctuary, O Lord; the place which Thy hands have established." He is watching over me now as surely as he watched over the children of Israel, keeping my fears at bay and assuring me of coming joy. In the midst of the Buddhist temples and the dirty politics and the rats, I am going to find a treasure.

Mark, we are a long way from that cracked-plaster room in Kramer Hall where together we began the pilgrimage that has landed me in this mighty 747. But God is near now, as he was then. And as I head for the distant shore, the words of this grand old hymn keep filling my heart:

> All the way my Savior leads me;
> What have I to ask beside?
> Can I doubt his tender mercy,
> Who through life has been my guide?
> Heavenly peace, divinest comfort,
> Here by faith in him to dwell!

For I know, whate'er befall me,
Jesus doeth all things well.
Amen!
I love you!!!

Love,
Hope

DATE DUE
